Praise for *The Digital Play*

CU00656526

'In today's tumultuous business environm
represents a no-nonsense guide to winning in a dynamic technology-
driven world. The book is filled with practical advice and straight talk on
what works and what doesn't work - the instruction manual we all need
to execute in order to be a successful digital company. It's a must-read
for every leader in your company, not just your technology leaders.'

John Marcante, former Global CIO of Vanguard;
current US CIO-in-Residence at Deloitte.

'*The Digital Playbook* provides practical, pragmatic and proven insights
for business and technology leadership. Eminently readable and
thoughtfully organised, it's a thought-provoking compilation of game
changing advice that I highly recommend as a must-read for anyone
involved in technology-related decision making in today's fast-paced
business environment.'

Stephen Fugale, former CIO of Villanova University,
Cigna Property and Casualty; CEO of Bernova

'*The Digital Playbook*'s timely and timeless unconventional wisdom
uniquely readies c-suites with the uncommon candor, courage and clarity
the tech-driven business world requires. It stands apart in delivering
the candid insights, practical guidance and due warnings leaders need
to accelerate digital strategy, forge lasting competitive edge and drive
lasting value. *The Digital Playbook* cuts through corporate stagecraft
and consultant double-speak to deliver ten candid strategic technology
lessons every c-suite needs to thrive.'

Noah Barsky, Professor, Villanova University

'*The Digital Playbook* is a valuable resource for understanding the
role that technology plays in business strategy, business models and
business processes. Steve provides a comprehensive overview of the
various technologies that can impact these areas and offers insights on
how to identify and track these technologies in order to leverage them for
competitive advantage. The emphasis on the importance of "matching"
technologies with business processes, business models and strategies

is particularly noteworthy, as is the focus on prototyping to measure the impact of these technologies. This book is a must-read for anyone looking to stay current on the latest technologies and how they can drive business success.'

Niraj Patel, Chief Information Officer at Greystone &
Co; former CIO at GMAC

'Infused with hard-won wisdom, this brilliant book is an invitation for leaders to accelerate achievement. *The Digital Playbook* is a gift to leaders in every industry. Steve Andriole has written a must-read primer for anyone considering digital endeavors. Read this book – and learn from one of the best. Steve is a unique and celebrated voice in strategic technology, innovation and entrepreneurship. The book is a remarkably practical, accessible and applicable text by a writer who deftly blends evidence and action. *The Digital Playbook* is an investment which will reap near- and long-term rewards. And it's delightful!'

David Henkin, Chief Innovation Officer at Vertex Inc.
(VERX, Nasdaq)

'*The Digital Playbook* should be required reading for any leader with a title that starts with C, for any size organization. I wish I could send this book to every CEO, CFO, COO, Chairman or government Secretary that I've ever worked with as a CIO. The lesson for leaders here is that business IS technology now, with the goals to create competitive advantage. The magic starts with being able to clearly articulate "What problem are we trying to solve?". I've been asking leaders this question for literally decades when presented with "We should buy this software" from a CEO or CFO. Steve's book does such a great job communicating why this is the question, and then understanding how to proceed, starting with business processes. This book will be on my C-Level holiday gift list for a long time.'

Aaron Weis, Chief Information Officer at Department
of the Navy

'*The Digital Playbook* is an enlightening reminder that strategic technology and business are completely intertwined and impact all industries. By following this guide, business leaders will be ahead of the curve. They will save time and money while generating competitive advantage, all of which are crucial to building and sustaining a successful business. Dr. Andriole's expertise is critical.'

Danielle McIntee, Senior Associate in Institutional Equity Sales at Raymond James

THE DIGITAL PLAYBOOK

Pearson

At Pearson, we believe in learning – all kinds of learning for all kinds of people. Whether it's at home, in the classroom or in the workplace, learning is the key to improving our life chances.

That's why we're working with leading authors to bring you the latest thinking and best practices, so you can get better at the things that are important to you. You can learn on the page or on the move, and with content that's always crafted to help you understand quickly and apply what you've learned.

If you want to upgrade your personal skills or accelerate your career, become a more effective leader or more powerful communicator, discover new opportunities or simply find more inspiration, we can help you make progress in your work and life.

Every day our work helps learning flourish, and wherever learning flourishes, so do people.

To learn more, please visit us at **www.pearson.com**

The Financial Times

With a worldwide network of highly respected journalists, *The Financial Times* provides global business news, insightful opinion and expert analysis of business, finance and politics. With over 500 journalists reporting from 50 countries worldwide, our in-depth coverage of international news is objectively reported and analysed from an independent, global perspective.

To find out more, visit **www.ft.com**

Stephen J. Andriole

THE DIGITAL PLAYBOOK

HOW TO WIN THE STRATEGIC TECHNOLOGY GAME

Pearson

Harlow, England • London • New York • Boston • San Francisco • Toronto • Sydney
Dubai • Singapore • Hong Kong • Tokyo • Seoul • Taipei • New Delhi
Cape Town • São Paulo • Mexico City • Madrid • Amsterdam • Munich • Paris • Milan

PEARSON EDUCATION LIMITED
KAO Two
KAO Park
Harlow CM17 9NA
United Kingdom
Tel: +44 (0)1279 623623
Web: www.pearson.com

First edition published 2023 (print and electronic)
© Pearson Education Limited 2023 (print and electronic)

ISBN: 978-1-292-44306-5 (print)
        978-1-292-44305-8 (ePub)

British Library Cataloguing-in-Publication Data
A catalogue record for the print edition is available from the British Library

Library of Congress Cataloging-in-Publication Data
Names: Andriole, Stephen J., author.
Title: The digital playbook : how to win the strategic technology game /
    Stephen J. Andriole.
Description: First edition. | Harlow, England ; New York : Pearson, 2023. |
    Includes bibliographical references and index. | Summary: "In today's
    tumultuous business environment, The Digital Playbook represents a
    no-nonsense guide to winning in a dynamic technology-driven world. The
    book is filled with practical advice and straight talk on what works and
    what doesn't work. It's filled with applied lessons for building the
    core competencies you need in order to win the technology war. The book
    comes at a time where enterprises are struggling to define their digital
    strategy, talent is being lost to digital natives and customer
    expectations demand nimble processes and seamless interactions.
    I challenge you to read and implement the practices outlined in The
    Digital Playbook. Share the lessons and action plans with your team.
    I have no doubt that you will look at technology in a different way and
    you will now have the gameplan to succeed in today's digital world"--
    Provided by publisher.
Identifiers: LCCN 2023000982 | ISBN 9781292443065 (paperback) | ISBN
    9781292443041 (ebook) | ISBN 9781292443058 (epub)
Subjects: LCSH: Information technology--Management. | Strategic planning.
Classification: LCC HD30.2 .A5353 2023 | DDC 658.5/14--dc23/eng/20230112
LC record available at https://lccn.loc.gov/2023000982

10 9 8 7 6 5 4 3
27 26 25 24 23

Cover design by Kelly Miller

Print edition typeset in 9.5/13, Helvetica Neue LT W1G by Straive
Printed by Ashford Colour Press Ltd, Gosport

NOTE THAT ANY PAGE CROSS REFERENCES REFER TO THE PRINT EDITION

CONTENTS

Pearson's Commitment to Diversity, Equity and Inclusion

Pearson is dedicated to creating bias-free content that reflects the diversity, depth and breadth of all learners' lived experiences. We embrace the many dimensions of diversity including, but not limited to, race, ethnicity, gender, sex, sexual orientation, socioeconomic status, ability, age and religious or political beliefs.

Education is a powerful force for equity and change in our world. It has the potential to deliver opportunities that improve lives and enable economic mobility. As we work with authors to create content for every product and service, we acknowledge our responsibility to demonstrate inclusivity and incorporate diverse scholarship so that everyone can achieve their potential through learning. As the world's leading learning company, we have a duty to help drive change and live up to our purpose to help more people create a better life for themselves and to create a better world.

Our ambition is to purposefully contribute to a world where:

- Everyone has an equitable and lifelong opportunity to succeed through learning.
- Our educational products and services are inclusive and represent the rich diversity of learners.
- Our educational content accurately reflects the histories and lived experiences of the learners we serve.
- Our educational content prompts deeper discussions with students and motivates them to expand their own learning and worldview.

We are also committed to providing products that are fully accessible to all learners. As per Pearson's guidelines for accessible educational Web media, we test and retest the capabilities of our products against the highest standards for every release, following the WCAG guidelines in developing new products for copyright year 2022 and beyond. You can learn more about Pearson's commitment to accessibility at:

https://www.pearson.com/us/accessibility.html

While we work hard to present unbiased, fully accessible content, we want to hear from you about any concerns or needs regarding this Pearson product so that we can investigate and address them.

- Please contact us with concerns about any potential bias at: https://www.pearson.com/report-bias.html

- For accessibility-related issues, such as using assistive technology with Pearson products, alternative text requests, or accessibility documentation, email the Pearson Disability Support team at: disability.support@pearson

ABOUT THE AUTHOR

Stephen J. Andriole is the Thomas G. Labrecque Professor of Business Technology at the Villanova University School of Business. He is also the CEO of TechVestCo, LLC through which he provides consulting services. He is formerly the Senior Vice-President and CTO of Safeguard Scientifics, Inc. and Cigna Corporation, and the Interim CIO of Shire Pharmaceuticals. He began his career at the Defense Advanced Research Projects Agency (DARPA) where he was the Director of the Cybernetics Technology Office. He was also a Professor of Systems Engineering at George Mason University and a Professor of Information Science & Electrical & Computer Engineering at Drexel University. He is the author of many books and articles on technology, management, emerging technology, venture, innovation and entrepreneurialism, all of which are documented at www.andriole.com

AUTHOR'S ACKNOWLEDGEMENTS

I've been influenced by all sorts of friends, colleagues, CEOs, chairpersons of boards, government officials, CIOs, CTOs, foundation presidents – you name it. If I named them all here, I'd no doubt leave some names off – names who thought they were more influential than they were, and those who had no idea they were influential at all. So, despite how much fun it would be to list all the major and minor technology celebrities who've appeared in my professional life, I'll forgo the exercise and acknowledge perhaps an unlikely source of inspiration: my undergraduate students at Villanova University who have impacted me and this book in so many ways. My ability to distil everything in this book is the result of so many classes where my students had no idea they were helping crystallise the message described here. But their answers to my constant questions – as well as their (almost always) excellent questions – completed the book. So, this book is dedicated to them. They keep me young, which is how they always are and always will be. Thanks everyone who endured my classes. I know I enjoyed them more than you. As always, I'd like to thank the Labrecque family for supporting me for so many years.

PUBLISHER'S ACKNOWLEDGEMENTS

05–06 Harvard Business Publishing: Carucci, Ron (2017). "Executives Fail to Execute Strategy Because They're Too Internally Focused." Harvard Business Review; **6 Baseline:** Cone, Edward (2002) "Blame Enough to Go Around at K-Mart." Baseline; **7 and 175 McGraw-Hill:** Adapted from Collis, David J., and Cynthia A. Montgomery. Corporate Strategy: A Resource-Based Approach. 2nd ed. Boston: McGraw-Hill/Irwin, 2005; **13 Software AG:** SofwareAG (2022). "What Is Process Mining?" SoftwareAG. https://www.softwareag.com/en_corporate/resources/what-is/process-mining.html; **15 Sparx Systems**: Adapted from Business Process Model and Notation (BPMN) retrieved from https://sparxsystems.com/enterprise_architect_user_guide/15.2/model_domains/bpmn_1_4.html; **17 Calvin Tan:** Based on Tan, Calvin (2014). "Business Processes." CALVINTKM; **24 TechTarget:** Pratt, Mary (2021) "Low-Code & No-Code Development Platforms." TechTarget, Mary K. Pratt; **25 David Taylor:** Taylor, David (2022). "Data Lake vs Data Warehouse: What's the Difference?" Guru99; **25 NetApp:** NetApp (2022). "What is a Data Fabric?" NetApp; **26 Andrew Overheid:** Overheid, Andrew (2022). "Understanding Fog Computing vs Edge Computing." Onlogic Blog; **27 CB Information Services, Inc.:** CB Insights. "Quantum Computing vs. Classical Computing in One Graphic.", https://www.cbinsights.com/research/quantum-computing-classical-computing-comparison-infographic/; **28 Dotdash Meredith:** Hayes, Adam (2022) "What is Blockchain?" Investopedia; **29–31 ZDNET:** Ranger, Steve (2022). "What is Cloud Computing? Everything You Need to Know About the Cloud Explained." ZDNet; **34 Gartner, Inc.:** Gartner Group (2022a) "Cybersecurity Mesh", https://www.gartner.com/en/information-technology/trends/; **35 Qualtrics:** Qualtrics (2022). "What is Social Media Analytics in 2022?" Qualtrics; **37 and 38 SAP:** SAP. (2022). "What is Augmented Reality?" SAP https://www.sap.com/insights/what-is-augmented-reality.html; **38 Encyclopaedia Britannica, Inc.:** Britannica (2022). Robotics. https://www.britannica.com/technology/robotics; **41 Take-off Professionals:** TOPS Marketing (2022). "Guide to 3D Modeling." Take-Off Professionals; **41 General Electric:** GE (2022). "What is Additive Manufacturing?" GE; **42 California Manufacturing Technology Consulting:** CMTC (2021). "Advanced Manufacturing, Additive Manufacturing, Future of Manufacturing: Top 8 Industries

Benefiting from Additive Manufacturing." CMTC; **42 SAP SE:** Morrow, Emily (2021) "Total experience: Definition, Benefits, Tips of TX." The Future of Customer Engagement & Experience."; **43 Humanperf Software:** Humanperf Blog (2021) "Will the Total Experience (TX) be the Key Trend for the Coming Decade?"; **44 Vox Media, LLC:** Welsh, Oli (2022). "The Metaverse, Explained." Polygon; **48 Calvin Tan:** Adapted from Tan, Calvin (2014) "Business Processes." CALVINTKM; **52 Salesforce, Inc.:** Salesforce (2022). "What is Digital Transformation." Saleforce.com; **53 Red Hat, Inc.:** The Enterprisers Project (2016). "What is Digital Transformation? The Enterprisers Project; **53 SAS Institute Inc.:** SAS (2022). "Digital Transformation: What It Is & Why It Matters; **53 ZDNET:** Samuels, Mark (2021). "What is Digital Transformation? Everything You Need to Know about How Technology is Reshaping Business." ZDNet; **56 Massachusetts Institute of Technology:** Andriole, Stephen J (2017). "Five Myths of Digital Transformation," Sloan Management Review; **59 SelectHub:** O'Shayghnessy, Kim (2016) "8 Reasons Why ERP is Important." SelectHub; **63 Dow Jones & Company, Inc.:** Deloitte (2022). "The Role of Culture in Digital Transformation." CIO Journal; **67 Deloitte AB:** van Duin, Stefan & Bakhshi, Naser. (2017). "Artificial Intelligence Defined." Deloitte; **68 IBM:** IBM (2020). "Supervised Learning." IBM Cloud Education; **69 A Medium Corporation:** Taniya (2018). "Machine Learning Algorithms: A comparison of Different Algorithms & When to Use Them Medium. https://medium.com/@taniyaghosh29/machine-learning-algorithms-what-are-the-differences-9b71df4f248f; **72 Ken Olsen:** Quote by Ken Olson; **72 MarketWatch, Inc.:** Vlastelica, Ryan (2017) "Automation Could Impact 375 Million Jobs by 2030." MarketWatch; **72 Bloomberg L.P:** Whitehouse, Mark. Sam, Cedric & Rojanasakul, Mira (2017). "Is Your Job About To Disappear? QuickTake" Bloomberg; **74 Yahoo Inc.:** Sozzi, Brian (2021). "McDonald's Automated Drive-Thru is Just the Latest Sign of Robots Taking Over Fast-Food." Yahoo Finance; **75 Interesting Engineering, Inc.:** Alexander, Donovan (2021) "9 Robots That Are Invading The Agriculture Industry." Interesting Engineering; **75 Honeywell International Inc.:** Honeywell (2021). "Why Companies Say Automation is a Top Goal." Honeywell; **75 University of Oxford:** The University of Oxford (2019). "AI Technology Can Predict Heart Attacks." Healthresearch; **76 LawGeex:** LawGeez (2017). "Comparing the Performance of Artificial Intelligence to Human Lawyers in the Review of Standard Business Contracts." LawGeez; **76 Hackernoon:** Sergeenkov, Andrey (2019) "Artificial Intelligence is Becoming Better than Human Expertise." HackerNoon; **76 Place Stars, Inc.:** Baral, Susmita (2021) "When Will Automation Take Over the Trucking Industry?" LA Times Blog; **77 IEEE:** From Andriole and IEEE IT Professional. Andriole, SJ (2022) "Automation is a

10-Step Competitive Necessity." Published in: IEEE IT Professional (Volume: 24, Issue: 1, 01 Jan. Feb. 2022) DOI: 10.1109/MITP.2021.3136017; **81 Changing Works:** Changing Minds (2017) "The Elements of the Conversation." Changing Minds http://changingminds.org/techniques/conversation/conversation.htm; **82 Forbes Media LLC:** Greyling, Cobus (2020) "Key Considerations in Designing a Conversational User Interface", Medium; **88–89 Trend Micro Incorporated:** Trend Micro (2020) "The New Norm", Trend Micro Research; **90 Ecosystm:** Team Ecosystm (2019) "Things you need to know about Cyber Attacks, Threats & Risks." Ecosystm; **92 IONOS Inc.:** Digital Guide Ionos (2022) "Social Bots – the Technology Behind Fake News." Digital Guide Ionos; **93 Shelly Palmer:** Palmer, Shelly (2018) "How to Build Your Own Troll Bot Army." Shellypalmer.com; **94 Webroot:** Webroot (2022) "What are Bots, Botnets and Zombies?" Webroot; **94 IDG Communications, Inc.:** Hill, Michael & Swinhoe, Dan (2021) "The 15 Biggest Data Breaches of the 21st Century." CSO; **95 Ecosystm:** Team Ecosystm (2019) "Things you need to know about Cyber Attacks, Threats & Risks." Ecosystm; **97 Wesley Chai:** Chai, Wesley. 2022 "Cloud Computing." TechTarget; **97 Krishna Narayanaswamy:** Quoted by Krishna Narayanaswamy; **98 Federal Communications Commission:** Westar (2022) "Top 10 Practical Cybersecurity Strategies for Businesses." Westar from Article Source: http://www.fcc.gov/cyberforsmallbiz; **99 Mansueto Ventures:** Alton, Larry (2020) "The 8 Best Cybersecurity Strategies for Small Businesses in 2021." Inc. Magazine; **100 BitSight Technologies, Inc.:** Shah, Samit (2021) "The Financial Impact of SolarWinds Breach." Bitsight; **100 CQ Roll Call:** Ratnam, Gopal (2021) "Cleaning up SolarWinds Hack May Cost as Much as $100 Billion." Roll Call; **102 Embroker Insurance Services, LLC:** Embroker Team (2022) "How Much Can a Data Breach Cost Your Business?" Embroker; **101 Forbes Media LLC:** Klebnikov, Sergel (2019) "Companies with Security Fails Don't See Their Stocks Drop As Much, According To Report." Forbes Magazine; **101 IDG Communications, Inc.:** Swinhoe, Dan (2022) "The Biggest Data Breach Fines, Penalties"; **102 Foresight Resilience Strategies, LLC:** Bobrow, Adam (2022) "Does Spending More on Cyber Mean less Risk?" Foresight Resilience Strategies; **107 PublicAffairs:** Zuboof, Shoshona (2019) The Age of Surveillance Capitalism: The Fight for a Human Future at the New Frontier of Power NY: Public Affairs; **111 Harvard Business Publishing:** Wessel, David (2018) "Is Lack of Competition Strangling the U.S. Economy?" Harvard Business Review; **111 Homeland Security:** Department of Homeland Security (2018) "Cybersecurity Strategy." Department of Homeland Security https://www.dhs.gov/sites/default/files/publications/DHS-Cybersecurity-Strategy_1.pdf; **113 FEDERAL BUREAU OF INVESTIGATION:** FBI

(2022) "White-Collar Crime." FBI; **113 ComplyAdvantage:** Comply Advantage (2022) "Cryptocurrency Regulations in the United States." Comply Advantage; **114 The New York State Society of CPAs:** Carmichael, Doug (2018) "Audit vs. Fraud Examination." CPA Journal; **114 Deloitte AB:** Deloitte (2022) "Fraud Policies." Deloitte; **115 Endeavor Business Media, LLC:** Kennedy, Joe (2018) "We're No. 25: Why the US Must Increase Its Tax Incentives for R&D." Industry Week; **115 Precisely:** Tozzi, Christopher (2021) "Top Regulatory Compliance Frameworks for 2021." Precisely; **116 Duke University Health System:** Duke Health (2022) "Lobbying Definitions, Exceptions, and Examples." Duke Health; **122 Industry Dive:** Eide, Naomi (2021) "4 Predictions for CIOs to Watch from Gartner." CIO Dive; **123 Software Advice, Inc.:** Montgomery, Olivia & Kumar, Rahul (2020). "What Is a RACI Chart?" Software Advice; **123–124 HubSpot, Inc.:** Erik Devaney October 06, 2022 "9 Types of Organizational Structure Every Company Should Consider." HubSpot; **134 Dotdash Meredith:** WILL KENTON, December 30, 2020, "What Is Commercialization, Plus the Product Roll-Out Process" Investopedia; **136 and 186 IEEE:** Adapted from Stephen J. Andriole, Automation is a 10-Step Competitive Necessity, IT Professional (Volume: 24, Issue: 1, 01 Jan.-Feb. 2022) IEEE; **146 Clayton Christensen:** Quoted by Clayton Christensen; **157 Dow Jones Tech:** Siegman, Alex (2018). "What is AI?" Medium, https://medium.com/dowjones/what-is-a-i-a49d298e6624; **160 McKinsey & Company:** "Tech Talent Tectonics: Ten New Realities for Finding, Keeping, & Developing Talent." McKinsey; **161 Fortune Media IP Limited:** Kidwai, Aman (2021) "How to find and hire the best tech talent in 2022." Fortune Magazine; **163 IDG Communications, Inc.:** Pratt, Mary & Florentine, Sharon (2022) "Employee Retention: 10 Strategies for Retaining Top Talent." CIO Magazine; **163 Fast Company & Inc.:** Marquet, Kristin (2022) "Six Ways to Retain Your Best Talent." Fast Company; **182 IEEE:** From Andriole and IEEE IT Professional. Andriole, SJ (2022) "Automation is a 10-Step Competitive Necessity." Published in: IEEE IT Professional (Volume: 24, Issue: 1, 01 Jan. Feb. 2022) DOI: 10.1109/MITP.2021.3136017; **188–189 Snopes Media Group Inc.:** Mikkelson, David (2022) "Dragnet: 'Just the Facts. Ma'am'." Snopes; **193 William Ockham:** Quoted by William of Ockham; **193 Leonardo da Vinci:** Quoted by Leonardo da Vinci; **193 William Shakespeare:** Quoted by William Shakespeare; **193 Mies Van Der Rohe:** Quoted by Mies Van Der Rohe; **193 Bjarne Stroustrup:** Quoted by Bjarne Stroustrup; **193 Antoine de Saint Exupéry:** Quoted by Antoine de Saint Exupéry; **193 Colin Chapman:** Quoted by Colin Chapman; **193 Albert Einstein:** Quoted by Albert Einstein; **193–194 List25 LLC:** H., Petr (2015) "25 Unbelievable Things Americans Believe." List 25. https://list25.com/25-unbelieavable-things-americans-believe/

PREFACE

SOUND BITES

Let's start this way. If someone asked you to describe *The Digital Playbook* after you read it, here are ten things I'd like you to say:

1. "Without a strategy, a business model and an inventory of 'as is' and 'to be' business processes, *all is lost* . . . he tells you *how* to develop a strategy, *how* to develop a business model and *how* to extract the processes that can be improved, automated, eliminated or invented with existing and emerging technology . . . *actual practical advice about things none of us are very good at* . . . "

2. "He's no fan of consultants who tell you how to run your business or list the technologies you should track . . . *he wants you to reclaim 'core' competencies* . . . he wants you to distinguish between 'brains' and 'brawn' where *you have the brains and consultants have the brawn* . . . he makes you think about how much we've outsourced over the years . . . *which he thinks is way too much* . . . "

3. "He argues that *operational technology is now just a commodity* . . . like bottled water you can buy anywhere . . . that there's no difference among ERP apps, BI platforms and cloud providers – no matter what your vendors, consultants or brothers-in-law tell you . . . so buy, standardise and then *focus on strategic technology* . . . "

4. "He wants *CIOs and CTOs to stay in the operational trenches* . . . they're not strategists, so we should stop expecting them to do something they can't – or don't want to – do . . . if you want real strategic technology leverage, find people who live and breathe it . . . "

5. "*He makes you answer 3 questions about each emerging technology*: what it is/why you should care/what you should do about it . . . *boils it right down* . . . very helpful, like how you should fire your programmers and replace them with low-code jockeys, slow-roll quantum computing and stop taking 'The Metaverse' seriously . . . "

6. "AI and machine learning are game changers . . . you better understand them . . . *and implement an automation plan . . .* "

7. "*He hates flat organisations* – and tells you why . . . *he loves hier-archies, accountability, actual work-products and no-emotion leadership* . . . you'd better listen to his advice about strategic technology leadership and management, especially when he talks about governance . . . "

8. "He reminds you that discipline is necessary to increase the odds of innovation success . . . he also reminds you that *commerciali-sation is the only innovation metric that matters . . .* "

9. "*He knows – despite what you probably believe – that you don't have the talent to compete in an all-digital world: all new recruiting and retention strategies are necessary* . . . lots of food for thought here . . . better plan an off-site with your HR team about how to fill the competency gaps – because they're growing . . . "

10. "The book is full of *'plays'* – how you should think and what you should do – which are worth the price of the book . . . the book is unusual, *full of proclamations **and** action plans* . . . rare to find in the same place . . . he also has a sense of humour and more than a little irreverence about what we all do for a living . . . "

Here's a bonus soundbite:

"Somewhere along the way, we all got a little confused about how difficult, complex and impossible this game is to win. *The Digital Playbook* describes plays that work and game plans that produce wins. If you read the book carefully, you'll win the business-technology game . . . if you don't, you'll lose . . . "

Here's another one:

"*Stop listening* to the pundits, professional analysts (who sell 'reports' and then try to land you as a client), vendors and marketeers who just love-love-love *SAP (Oracle, Gartner, Apple, Microsoft* and who knows who else) . . . *they all have vested interests – and they're not yours* . . . "

Here's the last one (I promise):

"The development of a winning strategic technology plan is as much about leadership and competency as it is about process . . . *so look in the mirror before taking the field – and over the shoulder at your team . . .* "

When you're done with *The Digital Playbook*, I hope this is how you describe it to friends, colleagues, vendors and consultants. Tell them that *The Digital Playbook* is one of the most unusual books on business technology you've ever read, and perhaps the most useful one you've ever experienced.

PERSPECTIVE

There are reasons why most technology projects fail. There are reasons why most of *your* technology projects fail. Sure, you may declare them all successful along some convoluted continuum. Or you've mastered the art of spin. But you and I both know you're not that good at business-technology strategy, that your business model is far from perfect and the business processes derived from the model and the strategy are missing, ill-defined and sometimes just plain wrong. We know you struggle with anything "to be", that forecasting is not a core competency. We know there are major talent gaps on your technology team, and we know there are executives in your company who have no idea what digital does or about its extraordinary competitive power.

Do you really want to talk about this?

We don't have to. Many companies chug along just fine with slow-to-moderate growth. Others have near-oligarchic footprints in specific industries – like cloud and social media – which essentially guarantees some level of growth, so long as the sector itself continues to grow (and the anti-trustors stay asleep). If you sit in one of these companies, you probably should spend more time on mergers and acquisitions (M&A) than process improvement. But everyone else should be thinking about strategies, business models, business processes and the technologies that enable profitable growth.

NO-NONSENSE EXPECTATIONS

I'm not sure what you expect from books like *The Digital Playbook*. Like you, I've read lots of them. Or maybe, like me, you already know they say the same thing – that technology is now more important to business success than ever before. We both know technologies like AI, machine learning, augmented reality and edge computing are important. We know that business processes need help and that technology can – with the right investments at the right time – improve, automate, eliminate and invent business processes that save money and make money. You know this too. But you don't know exactly how to leverage existing and emerging digital technology despite all the executive education certificates hanging on your wall.

The Digital Playbook will help.

This book cuts to the chase. It tells you what you need to hear. It tells you how to leverage digital technology as the world moves closer and closer to full-digital, when technology seamlessly enables transactions or, put more directly, how technology will facilitate revenue generation throughout the twenty-first century.

The Digital Playbook describes twenty-first-century technology management in the context of an ever-changing competitive environment increasingly driven by digital technology. The book addresses the disappearing gap between business and technology. It helps you navigate the national and global competitive landscape in no uncertain terms. The book is readable, at times blunt. The content is easily absorbed – or rejected – even if you're still under the hypnotic effect consultants manage so effortlessly.

The book comprises a set of short, no-nonsense "briefings" organised around ten themes grounded in reality, not theoretical aspirations about what should be done. The book can be read in parts, at different times, when you're frequently interrupted by the events of the day. While it's no beach read, it's a comfortable way to understand what's going on in business technology, what you need to know and what you need to do. Hopefully, you will find *The Digital Playbook* useful. I'd be surprised if you didn't.

Analysts, vendors, consultants and pundits all love to tell you how different things are today, that how you buy and use information technology – "IT" – isn't the way it was in the twentieth and even the early twenty-first century. There's nothing profound about these observations. *Obviously things are different today.* If you need someone to tell how different they are, you've already lost the game.

But there's a distinct feel to the changes that requires you to think about business and technology differently, as one. It's all-digital now, from how you run your company, to how you design your products and services, to how you innovate. I hope you know that the *Fourth Industrial Revolution* is well under way and the *Future of Work* has already arrived. Sure, you need the trains to run on time, but you'd better be thinking about new routes for the high-speed trains you're building.

EVEN WITH HEADWINDS

A major premise of *The Digital Playbook* is core competency. For decades, you've been told you need armies of consultants to tell you how your companies work and what you should do to be competitive. Guess what? You don't need armies of consultants. You need smart people *who work directly for you.* We'll talk about core competency throughout this playbook. (Infrastructure management is not a core competency; business process modelling is.)

But there are still headwinds. I will never forget when a Chief Financial Officer of a Fortune 100 company told a group of us at a corporate offsite that the internet was *"a fad that would be gone in a couple of years".* This CFO – to which technology reported – really believed what he said. He was filtering the future through the past, which is a strong nod to scepticism and incrementalism, which still, incredibly, after all these years, paralyses lots of companies from accepting the changes technology has already delivered – let alone the changes it will deliver in the next decade. It's amazing how much air cover still exists for perspectives like this. (At the same company, the CEO – to which the CFO reported – suggested the company ration email.) Even today, it's still possible for technophobes to work together to limit the role technology plays – and the money it costs. *"If it ain't broke, don't fix it"* is the mantra. It's hard to leave what's perceived to be working, even when it's not, even when the competition is executing a full-digital game plan. But the real problem is that "IT" was – and often still is – defined around laptops, servers, enterprise applications, databases and networks, regardless of where they reside.

The core problem is our lack of understanding of *strategic technology.* This misunderstanding of technology permeates most companies, even today. "Technology" enables operations, not strategy, though there's endless pressure on chief information and chief technology officers to be more strategic, which most of them simply cannot do (and an equal number don't want to do). You need to leave your understanding of "IT" completely behind (and for others to manage) and embrace an entirely new way to leverage technology. This journey is complicated by the pull of the past, by technology investments already made, by technical debt (which you should ignore) and by mindsets that constrain our ability to reimagine the role that technology should play in current, and especially future, processes, products and services. Just know that "technology" has two faces: an operational face and a strategic face and, despite articles in trade magazines, webcasts and conferences about technology's dual role, technology remains largely operational. Executives and managers who have looked at one face for most of their careers find it difficult, if not impossible, to see a newer face, even though the strategic face is the one that yields the most market share and revenue.

OPERATIONAL VERSUS STRATEGIC TECHNOLOGY

Ignore your vendors, consultants, friends and family who want to convince you that there are enormous differences among *AWS, Azure* and *Google Cloud*, that *SAP* is completely different from *Oracle*, and that *Tableau* is awesome compared to *Qlik* and *MicroStrategy*. None of this is true. *You – and all companies – stay with their operational hardware, software and cloud vendors not because they're differentiators, but because switching costs are so high.* It's like people who stay in their houses rather than move because moving is so traumatic. Are they happy in their houses? Sometimes, but often they're not. Do you love your hardware, software and cloud vendors? Probably not. But switching is traumatic, so you stay put.

But just remember that operational technology is now fully commoditised. There's no real difference among cloud providers, laptop manufacturers, BI software vendors, video teleconferencing applications, ERP applications or network configurations – and they're all for sale or rent from your favourite vendor only too willing to take your order. Operational technology is like bottled water; you can find it anywhere.

What does this really mean? It means there's relatively little competitive leverage gained from how well you replace laptops, which ERP application you deploy or which cloud vendor you select. The real leverage – *the only differentiator* – is strategic technology. How to play the strategic game is the skill few companies have, and the skill I'm going to describe here.

Remember that vendors and consultants want to design your entire game plan. They know what's best, right? Not even close. Do you really believe that consultants know *all* about technology, *all* about every vertical industry and how to *best leverage* technology for competitive advantage? Really? The same professionals – hopefully not you – who believe they need consultants to survive, are the same ones who endlessly complain about how expensive and ineffective their consultants are.

TECHNOLOGY IS BUSINESS/BUSINESS IS TECHNOLOGY

There's no distance between business and technology. You cannot make a technology decision without simultaneously making a business decision, and vice versa. All technology decisions – even operational ones – are business decisions, and all business decisions are technology decisions – period, and forever. This means that when you decide to move your data and applications to Amazon's Web Services, Microsoft Azure or Google's Cloud Platform, you're directly impacting your business. Remember the AWS outages that hit *Netflix, Slack, Ring* and *Doordash* (*The Guardian,* 2021)? Or when *Goldman Sachs* lost $100 million (*FinTech Futures,* 2013)? These events are not Black Swans. One group noted "the Pervasive IT Failure Problem in the Financial Services Industry" (2 Steps, 2020). *Visa, Bank of America, Barclays* – you name the bank – have all had massive technology failures, so make sure you look both ways before crossing the business-technology street.

Business processes and whole business models must change. You must improve them, automate them or just kill them altogether. But what do you replace them with? Which technologies make all this happen? Which are irrelevant to your primary, adjacent and new markets? These are the strategic decisions you'd better make well.

Whether you like it or not, your company is now and forever a strategic technology company. But, like the CFO I mentioned:

- If you filter the future through the past, you will fail.
- If you see technology as servers, databases and help desks, you will fail.
- If you believe emerging technology adoption can be cautiously managed, you will fail.
- If you think consultants will save you (OMG), you will fail.
- If you believe your team is ready for all this, you will definitely fail.

It's not just about cloud-native applications, edge computing, innovation, AI, new centres of excellence or digital transformation (whatever that means to you). Obviously, all these things are important, but it's *how* you seek digital nirvana that matters most.

It's how you strategise.

PLAYS

You will notice "Plays" throughout the book. They appear as tinted boxes. They're worth your time.

> **PLAYS**
>
> *Pay attention to these. They summarise and instruct. Sometimes they're short and sometimes they're long. If you get nothing else from this book, they will justify whatever you spend on The Digital Playbook.*

PLAYERS

When I say "you" and "your" throughout the book, I'm talking to everyone who makes business-technology decisions, which includes project managers, program management officers, directors, vice-presidents, senior vice-presidents, executive vice-presidents, chief innovation officers, chief technology officers, chief digital officers, chief information security officers, chief operating officers, chief financial officers and chief executive officers. Let's also include members of the board of directors and those who sit on advisory boards. While I think the contents here are valuable to programmers, architects and engineers – the professionals who occupy the operational technology trenches – the purpose of the book is to impact the decision-making crowd – the ones who decide how strategic money gets spent.

When you're done with *The Digital Playbook* – and after you share it with your team – you'll think about technology differently and, more importantly, you'll know how to develop a strategic technology game plan.

You will also know what *not* to do.

COACH

I've seen a lot in my career (https://andriole.com), which started at the *Defense Advanced Research Projects Agency – DARPA* (Wikipedia, 2022) for short. After *DARPA*, I started my own technology consulting company – *International Information Systems, Inc.* – that I sold five years after it launched. I "retired" to *George Mason University* as a Professor of Information Systems & Systems Engineering (where I held the George Mason Institute Professorship), and then *Drexel University* as a Professor of Information Systems & Electrical & Computing Engineering where I founded and directed the Center for Multidisciplinary Information Systems Engineering. After *Drexel*, I became the Senior Vice-President for Technology Strategy and Chief Technology Officer at *Cigna Corporation* (CI), an enormous insurance company. After *Cigna*, I went to *Safeguard Scientifics* (SFE) also as the Senior Vice-President for Technology Strategy and Chief Technology Officer. At *Safeguard* – an internet holding company – we directly or indirectly invested in over 300 companies, a bunch of which became IPOs. While at *Safeguard*, I also served as a Principal at *TL Ventures*, a venture capital firm where I conducted due diligence on prospective investments and occupied some of the firm's board seats. After *Safeguard*, I returned to academia as the Thomas G. Labrecque Professor of Business Technology at *Villanova University's* School of Business. Since then, I've founded and co-founded several technology consulting companies. Some of these companies were successful; most were not. One company – *ListenLogic* – had a real shot at success but fell off a cliff – or maybe it was pushed: there are way too many stories to describe here (maybe later). I also served as the Interim Chief Information Officer at *Shire Pharmaceuticals* before the company was acquired by *Takeda*. The consulting company through which I continue to consult – *TechVestCo, LLC* – is still alive and well. My consulting clients – nearly 100 of them to date – have provided a front-row seat to all kinds of business-technology challenges. These clients were and remain across a huge number of public and private vertical industries – and government agencies – of all shapes and sizes. Lest I sound hypocritical, my consulting has been anything but mainstream. Much of it has been "corrective", where I've been invited to inspect operational and strategic technology teams, structures and processes. Sometimes I've even been asked to fire consultants (but don't tell anyone). Along the way, I've published a bunch of books and articles. I write for *Forbes Magazine* and also for *IEEE IT Professional.* (You can reach me at steve@andriole.com, stephen.andriole@villanova.edu, https://andriole.com or through LinkedIn at https://www.linkedin.com/in/steve-andriole-b4a731/. You can track me on Twitter https://twitter.com/steveandriole and my articles at *Forbes Magazine* at https://www.forbes.com/sites/steveandriole/?sh=6aac8d601c88.)

Don't you think it's time I leverage all this for some good? I sure do.

FOREWORD

John Marcante

I've had the privilege of knowing Steve both personally and professionally for many years. He has had an incredible career that spans academia, government, financial services, venture capital and consulting. Steve has published over 500 articles and numerous books. He has a passion for technology and a disdain for hype, something we share in common. Steve is a truth teller and someone who writes and advises based on real-world experience. Dr Andriole, as he is known by his students at *Villanova University*, is a visionary who has dedicated his life to shaping the leaders of tomorrow. I'm glad Steve has put his effort and energy into solving another elusive business challenge – becoming digital.

Steve's focus on business and technology strategy along with his thought-provoking style has had a profound impact on me since we first met on the *Villanova* Technology Advisory Board decades ago. Steve's viewpoints, which may be controversial for some, are based on his unique perspectives and experience. He has seen the world of large public companies as the CTO of *Cigna*, he has driven successful start-up companies as a venture capitalist and the CTO of *Safeguard Scientifics* and he has advanced our nation's use of technology as the Director of Cybernetics Technology at the *Defense Advanced Research Projects Agency (DARPA)*. These experiences have given Steve a unique perspective in shaping strategy and helping the technology industry navigate complex challenges.

In today's tumultuous business environment, *The Digital Playbook* represents a no-nonsense guide to winning in a dynamic technology-driven world. The book is filled with practical advice and straight talk on what works and what doesn't work. It's filled with applied lessons for building the core competencies you need in order to win the technology war. The book comes at a time where enterprises are struggling to define their digital strategy, talent is being lost to digital natives and customer expectations demand nimble processes and seamless interactions. I challenge you to read and implement the practices outlined in *The Digital Playbook*. Share the lessons and action plans with your team. I have no doubt that you will look at technology in a different way and you will now have the gameplan to succeed in today's digital world. Steve dedicates the early part of the book to the importance of strategy and the role technology can play in driving success. *Vanguard's* early success was attributed to sound investing principles – low-cost, broad-asset allocation and a long-term perspective. As the investment world began to adopt these same time-tested principles, we set out to find the next differentiator and competitive advantage for the company. As Steve points out in Chapter 1, when it comes to strategy, a simple model works best. His five strategic steps, outlined in the first chapter, lay the groundwork for enterprise strategy, business models, processes and the transformational technologies needed to create a digital playbook. For *Vanguard*, we decided to use technology to disrupt the world of financial advice. Our objective was simple: we understood that investors felt paralysed given the complexity of navigating the financial markets. Financial advice was also expensive and contributed to high-profit margins for many advisory firms and the processes were slow and bureaucratic. Startups were beginning to attack this space but their solutions were targeted toward full automation without human interaction. Our solution needed to be fully automated but hybrid in the sense that an advisor could be inserted into the process at key inflection points for support and guidance. The service also needed to scale in order for the advice to be priced at a disruptive low cost. And the technology platform needed to work seamlessly across many countries in order to serve as many investors as possible. We settled on a number of transformative technologies including a cloud native, API-based financial advisory platform that heavily utilised AI/ML. Our strategy, business model, reinvented processes and technology where the basis of our digital solution. One that today is helping to democratise financial advice for millions of investors worldwide.

In Chapter 7, Lead, Manage and Govern the Right Game, Steve provides clarity on what it takes to lead effectively in today's technology-driven world. Two points in particular resonated with me. First, no one knows your company, your industry, your clients and your talent better than you. So don't outsource your strategy. External perspectives can be helpful but your internal leaders must have the strategic core competencies to drive your enterprise forward. Second, be careful how many chiefs you create. Vanguard chose to have one global chief information officer reporting to the chairman and responsible for all technology around the world. Organisational structure matters when your strategy and technology need to align. In our case, having a single global enterprise accountable for technology helped deliver effective and scalable solutions and helped create accountability and avoid silos.

Steve dedicates Chapter 9 to finding, retaining and rewarding talent. His passion for developing the leaders of tomorrow has had an impact on me and many of my peers. As the Global Chief Information Officer at *Vanguard*, a job I loved and was privileged to hold for nearly a decade, our mantra was to *be the best place to work for technical talent.* In fact, *Vanguard* has been named *Computerworld's* Top 10 Best Places to Work in IT for the last five years, most recently coming in at number four. When I assumed the CIO role in 2012, our technology organisation struggled with employee engagement. Here are a few lessons learned, which I can attest helped take our technical staff from laggards to leaders when it came to engagement. First, *demonstrate you care as much about your technical teams as you do about your clients.* If we have learned anything from the past few years, it is to expect the unexpected. We have endured a pandemic, suffered through social injustice and we are currently witnessing a horrific war in Ukraine. Amidst all of this uncertainty, there are ample opportunities for leaders to lead from the front and encourage team dialogue. At a minimum, checking in on individual team members as they struggle with today's challenges is a must for leaders who truly care about their team's well-being. Next, leadership matters – e*nsure your technical leaders are good people leaders and not just good technicians.* Finally, we know building a mission-driven organisation is a differentiator for any company – *evangelise your mission and align your technical teams to both your purpose and to real client outcomes.*

As you can see from some of the examples I've outlined, I have personally benefitted from Steve's ability to see through the glitter and get to the heart of applied technologies that add value for companies and customers. I have applied many of the lessons outlined in this book during my own career running businesses and global technology for Vanguard. *The Digital Playbook* is the instruction manual we all need to execute in order to be a successful digital company. In today's competitive world, every organisation has to create a culture that attracts and empowers teams, serves clients in a differentiated way and delivers solutions that add shareholder value. Easy to say, but extremely hard to execute. *The Digital Playbook* outlines the needed steps to be successful. From talent, strategy, operational excellence, governance and cyber, *The Digital Playbook* is a must read for every leader in your company, not just your technology leaders.

John Marcante is the former Global CIO of *Vanguard*, and the current US CIO-in-Residence at *Deloitte.*

CHAPTER 1

YOU NEED A STRATEGY, A BUSINESS MODEL AND PROCESSES – OR DON'T EVEN TAKE THE FIELD

CHAPTER SUMMARY

- *If you don't know your company's strategy, business model or business processes, you cannot leverage existing or emerging technology.*

- *Knowing how to develop a strategy, how to extract a business model from the strategy and how to identify the business processes that you can improve, automate, eliminate or invent with technology is the hard work you cannot avoid.*

- *You need to rethink your dependence on the consultants and vendors in your life. If you cannot strategise, build business models, identify, profile and mine business processes, track technologies and identify the business-technology matches that will make you more competitive, you will fail.*

BACK TO FORGOTTEN BASICS

It's impossible to optimise the business-technology relationship without a solid understanding of the business you're trying to improve. Whenever I give a technology speech or teach a technology class, I always start with something like, *"So, what are we trying to fix?"* Then I start with an analysis of strategy, models and processes, which usually triggers some yawns (or worse with students). If you're yawning now, it's time to wake up to the most important play of whatever game you're playing. (We'll get to the technologies soon enough.)

Research tells us that companies are bad at strategising, worse at business modelling and generally clueless about processes, which is why so many technology projects fail to impact the business. It reminds me of how do-it-yourselfers complain about how long it takes to set up a painting or plumbing project. Or how everyone hates to practise. Or how no one wants to exercise to stay healthy.

Let's start with some bad news: you don't have what you need to succeed. If I asked you for your business-technology strategy that everyone accepts and whose message is consistently communicated, the business model derived from the strategy, the processes that populate the model and the technologies most likely to improve, automate, eliminate or re-invent these processes, you'd look at me like I was certifiably insane.

Here's the picture, which looks more complicated than it is. Figure 1 is not an abstraction: it's a simple set of sequential steps.

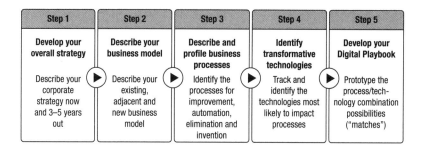

Step 1	Step 2	Step 3	Step 4	Step 5
Develop your overall strategy	**Describe your business model**	**Describe and profile business processes**	**Identify transformative technologies**	**Develop your Digital Playbook**
Describe your corporate strategy now and 3–5 years out	Describe your existing, adjacent and new business model	Identify the processes for improvement, automation, elimination and invention	Track and identify the technologies most likely to impact processes	Prototype the process/technology combination possibilities ("matches")

Figure 1 Five strategic steps

Listen: without a strategy, it's impossible to model your business. Without a model, it's impossible to define the processes and, without processes, it's impossible to match the technologies most likely to improve, automate, eliminate or reinvent processes. Please tell me if there's any other way I might communicate this differently.

There's something else that's important: core competencies (Twin, 2022). I know you've heard the term, though it was more popular a few years ago than it is today. But this is a good place to reintroduce the term and remove any ambiguity about its meaning.

Ask your vendors and consultants to cover their eyes while you study Figure 2.

Figure 2 challenges the consultant full-employment act which has been in effect for decades. During this time, companies have outsourced way, way too many essential business-technology tasks. Consultants have infiltrated all aspects of business and created an unprecedented dependency on their services which are often horrible (and always horribly expensive). When was it decided that outsiders could run companies better than insiders? I understand the default decision to go outside. Many companies decided it was easier to hire consultants to perform the tasks their employees could never perform. But why wasn't a root cause analysis performed? Why can't employees perform strategic tasks? Is it because the tasks are just too complex? Hardly. Is it because consultants own proprietary knowledge and experience? No. Is it because employees are incompetent? (Maybe, but not across the board.) These are root cause questions, but even these questions miss the point. Should outsiders *ever* perform insider tasks?

By the way, if you cannot strategise, build business models, identify and profile business processes, track technologies and identify the business-technology matches that will make you more competitive, what exactly is your job? I understand that Figure 2 looks like a vendor/consultant RIF

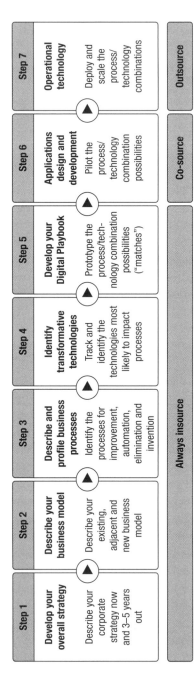

Figure 2 Business-technology core competencies

(reduction in force) – *because that's exactly what it is.* It's time to reclaim the core competencies that make you unique and competitive.

Let me pose a question. If a consultancy advises ten or fifteen firms in your industry (which it will no doubt claim as a unique qualification to engage your company), how is it possible for the same consultancy to provide anything unique to yours? Does the consultancy have that many tricks in its bag? Is there a unique trick for each manufacturing, healthcare, financial services, automobile – *any* – company on the planet? Proprietary strategies, business models and processes are yours and yours alone. If you must, think about Figure 2 as a homage to brains versus brawn, with a clear list of activities that require your brains and the ones that require the brawn of your vendors and consultants.

Brains versus brawn is a distinction that will determine your ultimate success. You must determine what you should know and what you can outsource as you develop your plays and game plan.

So how well would you do with the steps? Could you comfortably take them all? Do you agree with the 7-step sourcing continuum? If you don't, why do you have an actual company? Why not just engage a bunch of consultants to develop your strategy, build your business model, describe your processes, track technologies, match the processes with technologies, build the prototypes, develop the applications and enable all aspects of your strategic *and* operational existence? Trust me, they'd be happy to work with you. But you would lose the game.

YOUR SEARCH FOR STRATEGY

All strategic thinking is a "brains," not "brawn," core competency. You must own business strategies, business models and business processes. I say this as more and more companies are outsourcing their strategic vision – which is a huge mistake (and at least a minor embarrassment).

But there are problems.

A study in the *Harvard Business Review* (*Carucci, 2017*) – "Executives Fail to Execute Strategy Because They're Too Internally Focused" – makes the point:

> *"Many executives say they weren't prepared for the strategic challenges they faced upon being appointed to senior leadership roles . . . their focus is on internal issues: resolving conflicts, reconciling budgets, managing performance. Consequently, they pay less*

attention to external strategic issues like competitor moves, customer needs, or technology trends."

So, executives are too busy to strategise, don't know how to strategise and are too internally focused to even think about strategy. Does any of this describe you? The *HBR* research – and there's much more – describes the elephant in the room: companies don't strategise, and when they do their strategies are often useless.

You see the problem, right?

If you can't strategize, you cannot inform your business model, the processes that comprise the model, or the technologies that will improve, automate, eliminate or reinvent competitive processes. Translation? Without strategy → models → processes, you cannot win.

Everyone I know has developed a bad business-technology strategy. (I know even more who have no strategies at all.) Of course, they all believe they have enlightened strategies, or at least say so publicly. But, late at night, they know their strategic thinking is weak – or non-existent. You too?

At best, half-baked strategies are tiny flashlights in the darkness of business-technology uncertainty, a necessary tribute to the board of directors, a box for the CEO to check or, when public companies are challenged about their future, something the analysts who cover the stock can inspect. Sometimes supply-chain partners want to know what their partners plan to do with technology. But actionable? Hardly any of them are, and the ones that receive all the attention can cost a company millions if not billions of dollars. Just ask *Sears* (Torman, 2022), *JC Penny* and *K-Mart* about digital transformation driven by a business technology strategy. As Edward Cone (2022) notes:

> *"The profound failure of Kmart's ever-vacillating technology strategy was both a cause and a symptom of the problems that drove the retailer to bankruptcy."*

Making matters worse, Bughin et al. (2018) tells us that technology strategies fail because of process and purpose. They tell us that technology strategies are different from conventional business strategies (!) because technology moves so fast! They state that while incumbent business models are under constant threat, the *"majority of companies do not respond and ultimately fail".* In fact:

> *"Only 8% of companies believe that their business model will remain economically viable through digitalization."*

Strategic planning is an enormous industry, though "strategy" is defined in lots of different ways. There are blue ocean, good to great, playing to win, artistic and even safari strategies – and let's not forget the lords of strategy and the strategy paradox.

Who knew there were so many strategies? When I asked *Google "How many books on strategy have been published"*, I received this answer: *"about 1,750,000,000"*. In the same search, I noticed a link to the best 100 strategy books of all time (BookAuthority, 2022) and found titles like *Leap, Zag, Peak, Swipe* and *Obliquity*. I'm sure glad there's that much strategic advice out there. Aren't you?

What should you do?

Let's keep this simple, which means I'm not going to require you to reread Porter's Five Forces (Investopedia, 2022). Yes, it's a good piece of work, especially considering it was published in 1980. But lots of things have changed in four decades. I'm a huge fan – as you should be – of simplicity. When it comes to strategy, a simple model is better than one with multiple layers interpreted by hundreds of scholars, pundits and consultants over 40+ years.

Figure 3 is a simple model developed by David J. Collis and Cynthia Montgomery (2005). It comprises just three strategic elements: objective, scope and advantage. Remember that your strategy will yield a business model and your business model will yield the processes you're trying to improve, automate, eliminate or reinvent with existing and emerging technology.

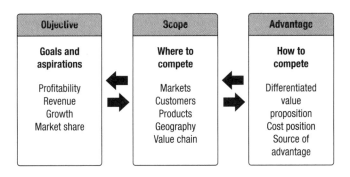

Figure 3 Elements of your business strategy
Adapted from *Corporate Strategy: A Resource-Based Approach* by David J. Collis and Cynthia A. Montgomery.

Can you develop a strategy with just three elements? Absolutely. Here are the questions you need to answer to define your strategy:

1. What's your *objective*? What are your goals and aspirations as defined by profitability, revenue, growth and market share? What percentage increases do you want? What *don't* you want? Do you want to grow your company – or sell it? What's your timeline?

2. What about the *scope* of your strategy? Where do you want to compete? Which existing, adjacent and new markets, customers and geography are you targeting? Products? Services? What do you want to sell to the target markets? What's the future value chain?

3. What's your *competitive advantage*? How will you compete in the product, service, market and geographic arenas you've identified? What's your differentiated value proposition, your cost structure and the sources of your market advantage? Why will customers buy what you're selling – and not what your competitors are selling?

The failures literature provides lots of reasons why business technology strategies fail. All of the usual suspects are there: diffuse objectives, poor management, lack of executive support, weak talent, too complicated, weak innovation culture, bad organisation, dysfunctional teams, budget issues and poor prioritisation, among other procedural and organisational problems. The only solution is a team of extremely talented in-house professionals. The timeline is three–five years out, noting, of course, that the further out you go, the less useful the strategy will be – unless you're really lucky.

This is real work. If you're unwilling to take some time, spend some money and assess your own strategic thinking, you can toss *The Digital Playbook* in the trash, get some coffee with a colleague or two, and discuss why the home team lost last night. If you're unable to do the work, you need to immediately find the talent that can. If it's not at hand, you need to spend the money to get the best strategists you can find.

The three–five-year window is aggressive because no one knows if Elon Musk will buy something that changes your revenue stream. Or if *Amazon* will buy *IBM*, or if tax policy will impact your R&D investment plans. No one knows if the world will be at peace in five years. Two–three years? Much better.

Key question: how proactive versus reactive do you want to be? You can proactively change your objectives, scope and advantage, which takes some courage. Or you can react to your traditional competitors. *Who do want to be?* The question cannot be answered without assessments around how volatile your industry is. But do you know how volatile your industry is today and how likely it will be tomorrow?

Default to volatility and proactivity.

The volatility/steadiness of any industry changes all the time. Was the real estate industry volatile during and after the pandemic? In the age of *Zoom, WebEx, Teams* and *RingCentral*, do you want to own lots of commercial real estate? What about energy? That equation changed when the Russians invaded Ukraine. Your strategy obviously must be flexible. The strategic planning process is continuous. *You need a talented, well-paid, permanent team that lives and breathes strategy (stop whining about how much talented people cost; just find them).*

My advice? *You should be more proactive than reactive. Imagine* major industry shifts in three–five years. But *address* immediate trends. Lead with business models and processes that will reimagine your business. Why? Because digital is making more and more industries volatile. Can you point to any truly "steady", "enduring" and "predictable" industries? No, you can't – including yours.

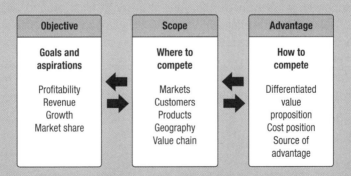

STRATEGY PLAYS

Strategic thinking is a core competency: if you can't strategise, you can't inform your business model, the processes that comprise the model, or the technologies that will improve, automate, eliminate or invent competitive processes.

When it comes to strategy, a simple model is better, like the Collis/Montgomery model consisting of just three elements: objective, scope and advantage.

Objective	Scope	Advantage
Goals and aspirations	**Where to compete**	**How to compete**
Profitability Revenue Growth Market share	Markets Customers Products Geography Value chain	Differentiated value proposition Cost position Source of advantage

Remember that your strategy will be converted into your business model and your business model will yield the processes you're trying to improve, automate, eliminate or invent with existing and emerging technology.

> *You can proactively change your objectives, scope and advantage, or you can react to your traditional competitors: you should be more proactive than reactive because no industry – not even yours – is immune to digital.*

BUSINESS MODELS

The shift from strategy to modelling is a natural one. A business strategy is a high-level plan of action to achieve market goals. It details alternative situations – best case/worst case scenarios – the business is likely to encounter, and the strategic actions it should take to achieve its goals under alternative scenarios. It also assesses the competitive landscape, since business strategies cannot exist in market vacuums.

A business model descends from the overarching strategy. It describes how a company plans to pursue its strategic objectives with go-to-market tactics likely to yield the largest market share and profits. Examples? Subscription models, direct sales models, franchising models, products-as-a-service models and retailer models, among others. Business models – like business strategies – are fluid: they can abruptly change, so companies must adapt to changing market conditions.

Business models comprise business processes, the specific steps that serve business strategies and enable business models. As such, business models stand between business strategies and business processes. Business models simultaneously look upward and downward where they must be faithful to the overall business strategy *and* house of the most effective processes.

Can you describe your business model? I wonder.

Hopefully, you've developed your strategy at least around objectives, scope and advantage. If you haven't, you cannot translate your objectives, scope and advantage into a model that defines your go-to-market plan.

Many companies use the Business Model Canvas to describe their business models. It consists of "elements" that include things like:

1. Key partners
2. Key activities
3. Key resources
4. Value propositions
5. Customer relationships
6. Customer segments

7. Channels

8. Cost structure

9. Revenue streams

It's just fine, though I always thought the canvas was missing an "element" on competition, especially new competition which we – and Michael Porter – often describe as "new entrants" (CFI, 2022).

While the canvas' elements seem almost elemental, most companies would fail a canvas test. Most executives would fail the test. Why? Because the work necessary to develop strategies, business models and process inventories is misunderstood and hard.

Would *you* fail the test?

Is the canvas too complex or not complex enough? Wrong question: the canvas is intended to stimulate thinking about how you make money. It also extends nicely from strategic objectives, scope and advantage – on the way to processes.

You must develop a business model. If I were standing next to you right now, I'd make sure you did the work. I'd also make sure you identified, described and profiled your existing (as-is) and future (to-be) processes.

BUSINESS PROCESS MODELLING, MINING AND MANAGEMENT (BPM³)

Again: each element of the Business Model Canvas should be comprised of existing processes that together describe how you do what you do. They're also the source of new processes that describe how you think you can make money in the future.

If you can't describe your business model, you can't identify existing processes in need of improvement, automation, elimination, or any new processes that, when enabled by the right technology, might improve your competitive position in the market. Is there a better way to communicate this? Not really. It's elemental.

But here's what you probably don't have, especially if you don't have a coherent business strategy:

- A flexible business model.
- An inventory of processes that define your business model.
- An inventory of the processes that cost you the most money and time.

- A real-time database of all of your business processes rank-ordered by their cost, profitability or other metrics.

- An inventory of all of your business processes in a single, integrated database.

- Databases of your processes rank-ordered by their candidacy for improvement/automation/retirement/reinvention with existing or emerging technology.

- Candidate new processes rank-ordered by their potential and, therefore, their location in the prototyping queue.

- Annually funded full-time teams – your own teams (not consultants) – who spend their lives modelling and profiling processes with the best business process modelling/management (BPM) tools.

The number of companies that have process databases is very small, so don't feel too bad about flying blind. Everyone flies blind. While business process modelling, management and mining are discussed at all kinds of conferences every year, they fail to occupy mainstream positions in most companies.

Yes, there's always a business unit or two that have piloted BPM[3] tools and techniques. But teams of BPM[3] professionals with annual budgets and seats at the big table? Hardly ever.

BUSINESS PROCESSES

Let's dig a little deeper. What's a business process? It's a set of organised activities, steps or tasks that people (or machines) undertake to achieve a specific result.

Business processes can be internal or external. Some explain how a company works and some explain how a company interacts with customers or clients.

Ideally, business processes are "modelled" in some specific order complete with all of the steps necessary to implement a task.

BUSINESS PROCESS MODELLING

How about business process *modelling*? Business process modelling (BPM) is a process unto itself. It's a process that "converts" business processes into models that can be assessed according to a number of criteria, such as cost, complexity and automation readiness. BPM is conducted by business analysts who implement the processes day in and day out.

BUSINESS PROCESS MINING

What about business process *mining?*

"Mining" is just that – the search for valuable assets which in this case are inefficient business processes that with the right technology can be improved, eliminated, automated or completely reinvented. Process data is inspected for what it reveals: how long does the process take? How expensive is it to implement? How inexact is it? How might time and money might be saved if the process was re-engineered? Process mining can yield gold. The identification of troublesome processes points directly to improvement, elimination, automation or reinvention. Many of the process vendors enable mining with toolsets. As always, select a tool and standardize it throughout your company.

BUSINESS PROCESS MODELLING AND MINING TOOLS

I assume you're at least vaguely aware of business process modelling/management tools and platforms. Some of these are well known and have been in the market for years, such as platforms from *Mendix, Appian* and *UiPath*. They enable business process modelling and mining.

I've been assuming – for good reason – that you should invest in business process modelling (BPM) tools that have their own notation (BPMN).

But there are lots of methods for describing business processes, including:

- Business process modelling notation (BPMN)
- Unified modelling language diagrams
- Flow charts
- Data flow diagrams
- Gantt charts

- Integrated definition for function (IDEF) modelling
- Petri Nets/coloured Petri Nets
- Object-oriented methods
- SIPOC diagrams
- Value stream mapping
- IPO model
- PERT diagrams
- Functional flow block diagrams . . .

Should you care about these? Not much, but you might hear someone on your team ask a question about one or two of them (so, now you have the list and the history of how business process have been described over the years). But, like climate change, it's settled history: BPM is the winner (though the climate lost big).

*You need to pick one platform – BPM (business process modelling with its notation [BPMN]) – and then pick one BPMN software tool and standardise it throughout your company – **no exceptions**.* Sure, you can acquire/lease and support five different BPM platforms, which makes no sense (which wouldn't be the first time technology decision-makers made decisions that made no sense). Just make sure the standardised platform's output integrates with your other software platforms. Ideally, the modelling platform integrates with, or within, the mining platform you select.

BPM^3 AT WORK

Make no mistake, BPM^3 is a discipline that can be applied to all of your internal processes and all of the external ones. BPM^3 describes your processes and identifies the processes that need help. Look at two examples. The first (in Figure 4) is a generic process model, while the second (in Figure 5) is a business process that describes the loan approval/rejection process.

Are there any aspects of the process that might be improved, automated, reinvented or eliminated? Could the loan application process itself be automated? Could the loan analysis process be automated?

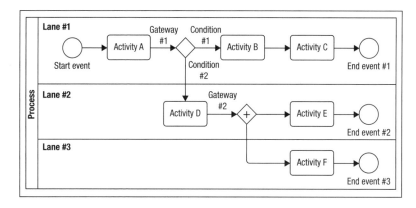

Figure 4 Generic BPM structure

Technology presents multiple opportunities to redefine processes – as Figure 6 suggests.

Companies with sophisticated process modelling and mining capabilities have a huge advantage over those that don't. But there are very few sophisticated BPM[3] companies. Where are you on the BPM[3] continuum? Do you track, model and mine business processes? (I doubt it, and it's costing you money.)

BMP[3] requires investment and discipline – lots of discipline. But the reward is enormous. So why doesn't everyone commit to BPM[3]? Part of the reason is because BPM[3] is initially time-consuming. But once a methodology, notation and tool are selected and standardised, the rest is about talent, funding and execution. Investments in (1) strategy, (2) business modelling and (3) BPM[3] are no-brainers: if you cannot define your strategy, your business model and the "as-is" and "to-be" processes that make you competitive, the game is lost before it begins.

BPM[3] is a discipline and methodology that permits anyone to model, modify and simulate business processes (that together comprise your business model). To assist these efforts, there are lots of proprietary and open-source cloud-based BPM[3] software tools that enable modelling and simulation.

Note that business process mining inevitably leads to process improvement/automation/elimination/reinvention which, in turn, leads to robotic

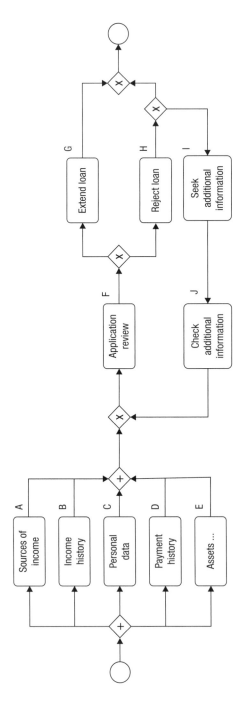

Figure 5 Loan approval/rejection process

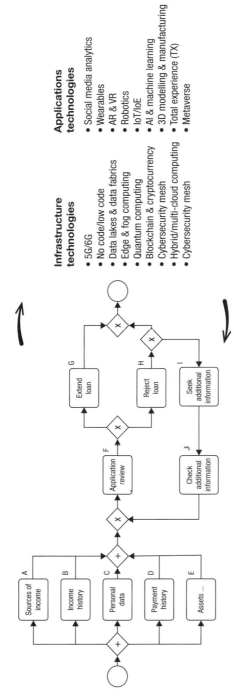

Infrastructure technologies

- 5G/6G
- No code/low code
- Data lakes & data fabrics
- Edge & fog computing
- Quantum computing
- Blockchain & cryptocurrency
- Cybersecurity mesh
- Hybrid/multi-cloud computing
- Cybersecurity mesh

Applications technologies

- Social media analytics
- Wearables
- AR & VR
- Robotics
- IoT/IoE
- AI & machine learning
- 3D modelling & manufacturing
- Total experience (TX)
- Metaverse

Figure 6 Business process improvement with technology

process automation – RPA (Olavsrud and Boulton, 2022) – and RPA leads to AI and machine learning, which will be discussed in detail in Chapter 4.

AFTERTHOUGHTS

I started this chapter with the yawns that follow strategic work. In my experience, yawns are often the least offensive reaction I get when I suggest that, without strategy, business models and the business processes that describe the models, all is lost. I cannot emphasise the importance of strategic work more. While everyone wants to get to the technologies that offer great promise – which many of them do – without a strategic compass, you have no idea how to leverage the technologies. Please remember that all good coaches need game plans comprising well-executed plays by talented professionals.

You've been coached.

BPM³ PLAYS

Many companies use the Business Model Canvas to describe their business models; you should too. Each element of the Business Model Canvas comprises existing processes that, together, describe how you do what you do. They're also the source of new processes.

If you can't describe your business model, you can't identify existing processes in need of improvement, automation, elimination, or any new processes that, when partnered with the right technology, might improve your competitive position in the market.

You need to pick one platform – BPM (business process modelling with its notation [BPMN]) – and then pick one BPMN software tool and standardise it throughout your company – no exceptions.

*BPM³ is a **discipline** that can be applied to all of your internal processes and all of the external ones. BPM³ describes your processes and the processes that need help.*

Investments in (1) strategy, (2) business modelling and (3) BPM³ are no-brainers: if you cannot define your strategy, your business model and the "as-is" and "to-be" processes that make you competitive, then the game is lost before it begins.

CHAPTER 2

TRACK AND PROTOTYPE THE PROCESS/ TECHNOLOGY MATCHES

CHAPTER SUMMARY

- *The technologies that impact your strategy, business model and business processes must be continuously identified and tracked.*

- *Three questions apply to each technology:*

  - *What's the technology?*

  - *Why should you care?*

  - *What should you do about it?*

- *The essence of strategic leverage is the "matching" of potentially impactful technologies with business processes, business models and sometimes whole business strategies.*

- *Technology/process matches should be prototyped to measure the impact technologies have on business processes and sub-processes. "Matching" is a core competency. Sometimes it works; sometimes it doesn't – but you must own it.*

TECHNOLOGIES YOU SHOULD TRACK

Pundits, industry analysts and consultants all have lists of technologies they believe you should track for competitive advantage. The lists change all the time because the industry "rejects" technologies, because investors move on, because companies decide the potential is not what they hoped, the technologies go mainstream or they're – *you're* – just unwilling to spend any money to dig deeper.

The most important aspect of the technologies is the impact they might have on your business processes, your business model and even your overall business strategy. But that's to be determined as you inspect your "as-is" and reinvent your "to-be" processes.

Some of the technologies could disrupt your business, while some might only offer opportunities to incrementally change things. Do you know which ones do what? Ultimately, business impact has two faces: save money and make money. If you're going to chase outcome metrics, these are the two to chase. (They're also the easiest to sell inside – to C-suiters – and outside – to stakeholders, shareholders and industry analysts – even if the details are sometimes fuzzy.)

But the path to these metrics goes through business models and processes – which are anchored in strategy.

Figure 7 lists the technologies you should be tracking. At the very centre are the business processes and models that define the essence of leverage.

Two kinds of emerging technologies are listed in Figure 7. The inner circle identifies enabling "infrastructure" technologies while the outer circle identifies the technologies most likely to yield technology-enabled applications. Note that the list assumes a team is always tracking technology trends. No matter how sceptical or cheap you may be (!), you'd better "officially" track technology trends with a well-funded team with access to senior technology decision-makers.

Some of these technologies are already on your radar. You're already using some of them. But there are many you've just begun to inspect, or "old" ones – like cloud computing – *morphing as we speak.* It's the morphing part that will sting you.

"Tracking" technologies is a never-ending job. If you underinvest here, you will lose the game before the whistle blows. Yes, tracking is real, continuous and influential – and the bridge to business models and processes, and sometimes even whole business-technology strategies. Remember that without strategy, technology has nowhere to go; without technology, strategy has no purpose.

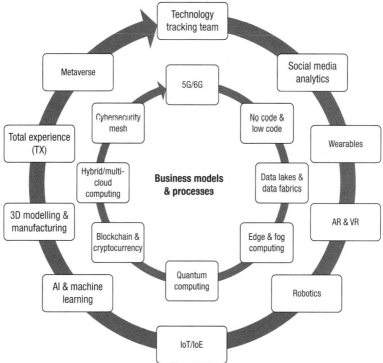

Figure 7 Technologies you should track

A quick test: how many of your technologists understand the full range of machine-learning algorithms and can discuss their strengths, weaknesses and the problems to which they're best suited? Or the hierarchy of neural network algorithms? Or the range of low-code platforms available for application development? Can they describe distributed ledgers? Or why data lakes are superior to data warehouses? This is where consultants claim to live (though seldom do). You *must* develop technology expertise. You should not cede this mission to consultants or analysts – or anyone with a vested interest in the advice they dispense. (How did you do with the test?)

The challenge is to assess evolving and new technologies with specific reference to *existing* business process, products and services and – much more importantly – to *new* processes, products and services. These assessments need to be objective – and not conducted by technology partisans whose children are majoring in – for example – AI and machine learning – where every problem is now an AI problem. If your world works that way, it's time to move.

Stare at Figure 7 for three minutes – not three seconds, but three minutes – and then ask yourself three questions about each of the technologies:

1. What is it?
2. Why should I care?
3. What should I do about it?

You should be able to answer all three and, despite what you may have been told, you don't need an army of professionals or consultants to tell you what to think or do about these technologies. You need in-house professionals who really understand your business model and where it should – or should not – go, and the technologies that will take it there. If you don't have these people, you should start recruiting and rewarding them immediately. Why? How could a consultant understand your business better than you (unless he or she is an ex-employee with a ton of experience in your industry)? Regarding the technologies, make sure you have in-house professionals who understand the essence and trajectory of each one. Don't rely on outsiders to explain your business or the technologies it needs to profitably grow.

The core questions should not focus on what makes the technologies work at the most basic level. There's brawn out there that can help explain how many sensors it takes to manoeuvre a self-driving car. What you need to understand is the essence of the technology, the features and capabilities that can improve your competitiveness. You need to understand the role that sensors play in autonomous driving and how sensors might impact your processes, products and services, not sensor circuitry. Huge difference.

As we begin the technology tour, let's stipulate that the technologies on the list are not the only technologies you need to track. Some of them will fade from importance in a few years or, more likely, just get embedded into your daily computing life. The relevance of quantum computing, for example, will likely be delayed, and the hype around "the metaverse" will quiet itself as definitions and progress disappoint developers and investors. But remember that all of the technologies on the list today are changing. For example, what you know about cloud computing today is almost irrelevant to tomorrow's cloud capabilities. It's the same for blockchain/cryptocurrency, especially if it goes mainstream. Your understanding and application of the technologies will be as fluid as your business processes.

Let's start with the infrastructure technologies that enable business processes and whole business models. Note the three questions throughout the tour.

INFRASTRUCTURE TECHNOLOGIES

5G/6G

What are they?

5G and 6G wireless communication is about speed, latency and security, and their relationship to your existing and future business models and processes. Their value lies in the impact they might – or might not – have on market share and profitable revenue.

5G is fast with little or no latency; 6G will obviously be faster. Availability and security, however, cannot be taken for granted.

Why should you care?

You should care about availability, speed, latency and security, in that order. But be sceptical about rollout schedules: providers talk good games – advertise even better ones – but rollout schedules are inconsistent and incomplete. Also make sure the devices on which your (and your clients') 5G/6G applications run are compatible through your customer applications (which you need regardless). Speed and latency should always be a concern, especially if any of your (streaming) products and services will be impacted by the capabilities of 5G and eventually – before the end of the decade – 6G.

What should you do about them?

Assess your products and services to determine the impact that speed, availability and security might have on them. Not much? Fine, look for communications technologies with greater potential. But if impact is potentially meaningful, then start to migrate your applications. 6G? Down the road, but anticipate more speed, availability and – perhaps less – security. Ask your network and communications vendors to prepare White Papers on their understanding of 5G and 6G and what they believe they can provide your company that will make it faster, more available and secure. Ask your internal team to prepare a strategic White Paper. Also – as always – study what your competitors are doing.

NO-CODE/LOW-CODE PLATFORMS

What are they?

This trend is a tsunami you cannot – *and should not* – avoid. Estimates project that "programming", as we've been conditioned to understand it, will disappear in less than a decade (except the programming necessary to develop low-code and no-code platforms). Does this mean that programming will completely disappear? No, but it does mean that huge parts of applications development will be with low-code/no-code platforms by "developers" with no formal programming training. I'd repeat this if it was necessary, but it sure shouldn't be.

So, what are low-code and no-code platforms (Pratt, 2021; note my **bold**)?

> *"Low-code/no-code development platforms are types of visual software development environments that allow enterprise developers and citizen developers to drag and drop application components, connect them together and create . . . apps . . .* **low-code and no-code modular approaches let professional developers quickly build applications by relieving them of the need to write code line by line.** *They also enable business analysts, office administrators, small-business owners and others* **who are not software developers to build and test applications.** *These people can create applications* **with little to no knowledge of traditional programming languages."**

Why should you care?

It's impossible to overstate the impact of low-code/no-code platforms *that enable non-programmers to develop applications.* (Note: low-code platforms are more powerful than no-code ones, but they both enable rapid application development.) Your team can develop applications faster and more cost-effectively than traditional requirements-driven programming-based application development. Just imagine what happens when "programming" – the quintessential bottleneck – "disappears". You'd better care about this trend if you want to save serious money and make money from the applications you can develop, launch and scale faster than ever before.

What should you do about them?

Low-code/no-code platforms are game-changers. You can now stop begging expensive programmers to join your company; you can actually reduce the number of programmers you house and feed. You should replace them with low-code/no-code platform jockeys, many of which can be your old programmers, but many will not. Assess the capabilities and desire of your programmers to transition. Some will and some won't want to take the journey. Expand the low-code/no-code expertise beyond the technology department and spread it across your business analysts – your subject matter experts (SMEs). You will save tons of time and money. The technology industry has handed you a gift. Accept it with a big smile.

DATA LAKES AND DATA FABRICS

What are they?

You should see data lakes and data fabrics as enabling all forms of analytics (Taylor, 2022; the **bold** is mine):

> "A **Data Lake** is a storage repository that can store a large amount of structured, semi-structured, and unstructured data. It is a place to store every type of data in its native format with no fixed limits on account size or file. It offers a large amount of data quantity for increased analytical performance and native integration . . . (a) **data lake is like a large container which is very similar to real lake and rivers.** Just like in a lake, you have multiple tributaries coming in; similarly, a data lake has structured data, unstructured data, machine to machine, logs flowing through in real-time."

> "A data fabric (NetApp, 2022) is . . . a **set of data services** that provide consistent capabilities across a choice of endpoints spanning hybrid multi-cloud environments . . . it . . . **standardizes data management practices** . . . across cloud, on premises, and edge devices."

Why should you care?

In the twentieth century, we had databases, which became data warehouses that are now data lakes optimised through data fabrics. Since most data is unstructured, you have no choice but to build data lakes; you have no choice but to analyse unstructured data for competitive survival. Why? It's impossible to perform analytics on just structured data when most data today is unstructured. Architecturally, you want a data infrastructure that enables flexible data analytics. You cannot compete without such a platform.

What should you do about them?

Data lakes are non-discriminatory data repositories that enable data analytics of all kinds of data. Data fabrics speak to an overall analytics philosophy – which you should adopt. Pilot tomorrow. There are lots of tools that will help you get this done. Start with your current data providers. See what they've got. If you're not impressed (through actual due diligence), move on, but remember that, long term, you need data lake/data fabric brains. You can leave the brawn to someone else. Never forget that brains are differentiators, and brawn's a commodity, but in this case very necessary brawn.

EDGE AND FOG COMPUTING

What are they (Overheid, 2022)?

> *"Essentially* (edge and fog computing) *. . . are enablers of data traffic to the cloud . . . edge computing happens where data is being generated, right at 'the edge' of a given application's network. This means that an edge computer connects to the sensors and controllers of a given device* (like a PC) *and then sends data to the cloud.*
>
> *"Fog computing is a compute layer between the cloud and the edge. Where edge computing might send huge streams of data directly to the cloud, fog computing can receive the data from the edge layer before it reaches the cloud and then decide what is relevant and what isn't."*

Edge and fog computing constitute a computing architecture that extends your cloud capabilities.

Why should you care?

There are benefits to edge and fog computing including especially speed and reduced latency in applications that require real-time processing (like military, autonomous vehicles and gaming applications), cost savings around data storage and movement, reliability even when clouds crash (in the same way you can still use your computer when your internet connection dies), better security by decentralising data, and scalability by simply adding more devices to the edge of the computing cloud.

What should you do about them?

The metrics above are your guide. Pilot edge/fog computing to determine the extent to which they deliver speed, cost savings, reliability, security and scalability. While you and your providers will never abandon centralised cloud computing, there are opportunities to "share" computing with edge/fog architectures. The key is to know how to share edge/fog and centralised computing for the greatest benefit – the end game. Your network vendors should be able to help here, but I'd also look first to your own internal networking and communications brains for guidance.

QUANTUM COMPUTING

What is it?

This technology is not ready for prime time – yet. Will it be? Yes, but no one knows exactly when. Here's a definition of quantum computing that focuses on the difference between more classical computers and quantum computers (Frankenfield, 2021):

"Quantum computers process information differently. Classical computers use transistors, which are either 1 or 0. Quantum computers use qubits, which can be 1 or 0 at the same time. The number of qubits linked together increases the quantum computing power exponentially. Meanwhile, linking together more transistors only increases power linearly.

"Classical computers are best for everyday tasks that need to be completed by a computer. Meanwhile, quantum computers are great for running simulations and data analyses, such as for chemical or drug trials. These computers must be kept ultra-cold, however. They're also much more expensive and difficult to build."

Why should you care?

If you're in the drug discovery/design, weather forecasting, computational chemistry, cryptography, complex financial modelling, or logistics business, you should care sooner rather than later. If you're not in these businesses, you don't need to care all that much until quantum computing begins to impact your business – and for that you'll have a lot of lead time to prepare.

I say this in spite of all the hype around quantum, which is growing every day. Remember whose vested interests hype serves. Quantum represents a new revenue stream for creators, developers and consultants. Position it – and all of the emerging technologies – accordingly.

What should you do about it?

If you're not in the above-listed industries, track it, that's all. If you're in those industries, start partnering with the major quantum vendors. The 2020s will reveal some major progress with selected applications. *Google* says it will be "ready" by 2029; *IBM* promises a shorter schedule. Time will tell. (The trade articles are fun to read – and the science fiction is even better. Remember the movie *iRobot*? It was incredibly prescient. Made in 2004, it points to a still unrealised future, the way quantum is described today.)

BLOCKCHAIN

What is it (Hayes, 2022b)?

> *"Blockchain is a type of shared database that differs from a typical database in the way that it stores information; blockchains store data in blocks that are then linked together via cryptography . . . as new data comes in, it is entered into a fresh block. Once the block is filled with data, it is chained onto the previous block, which makes the data chained together in chronological order . . . different types of informa-tion can be stored on a blockchain, but the most common use so far has been as a ledger for transactions . . . in Bitcoin's case, blockchain is used in a decentralized way so that no single person or group has control – rather, all users collectively retain control . . . decentralized blockchains are immutable, which means that the data entered is irreversible."*

Why should you care?

The financial industry will lead the way in the application of blockchain. Healthcare will follow. Blockchain will completely free itself of its singular cryptocurrency identity by 2025. It will become a legitimate transaction platform that mainstream technology vendors and vertical industry leaders deploy, such as what's happening now with the non-fungible token (NFT) industry – you know, the one that sells Melania's eyes and Tom Brady's memorabilia (though Melania's debut was pretty embarrassing [Armstrong, 2022]). If you're in the financial services or healthcare industries, you must track and pilot this technology immediately. But all that enthusiasm should be tempered somewhat by the blockchain mining process that currently consumes enormous resources that raises some environmental red flags you should also track (Kim, 2022).

What should you do about it?

Track and pilot immediately, especially if you're in the early adoption industries. Watch the mining process too, as well as the relationship between transactions planned for the metaverse, and blockchain as *one* of the major enabling technologies. Track the other challenges too, like scalability, latency, privacy, security and regulation. There's a lot going on here so don't be too easily seduced. Watch, pilot and deploy carefully. Start with your data professionals. If they're weak in the area, get some help. Your cloud providers offer "blockchain-as-a-service". Go there. There's also a "blockchain-as-a-service" (Sant, 2021) industry well beyond what cloud providers are offering. Start somewhere, but start.

CLOUD COMPUTING

This technology is your infrastructure, applications *and a major part of your technology strategy.* You must understand and exploit all aspects of it. *There are no exceptions to this advice.* So, let's dig much deeper than we have with the other technologies, which is perhaps surprising to you since you're already in the cloud with much of your infrastructure and many of your enterprise applications. You're also already offering your products and services through cloud providers, who have near-perfected the "as-a-service" strategy – to make as much money as they can.

The reason for the depth is simple. If you do cloud wrong, you will harm your business. If you do cloud really wrong, you could kill your business. The threats increase annually as cloud architectures and configurations change dramatically, and clients – you – are bombarded with features and capabilities that are both real and exaggerated. So pay attention.

First, the basics, which I suspect some of you have forgotten.

What is it?

Let's start with the basics. Cloud computing is the outsourcing of computing to a commercial vendor responsible for maintaining – "hosting" – data, applications and the tools that enable new applications development. It's "on-demand," which means you use what you need when you need it. It also enables customers to access the applications you sell. Software companies sell all sorts of "services" including customer relationship management (CRM), enterprise resource planning (ERP) and special purpose applications you've developed to support typical and specialized corporate activities, like marketing and innovation. Cloud computing represents freedom for some companies who have maintained their own data centres for years.

The cloud includes Infrastructure-as-a-Service (IaaS) which consists of servers, networks and storage. Platform-as-a-Service (PaaS) builds upon IaaS with platforms and tools that enable application development. Software-as-a-service (SaaS) is how applications are delivered internally to your employees and externally to your customers. When most of us think about cloud computing we're thinking about SaaS. Remember that all "as-a-service" capabilities require access to cloud providers' technology.

Many companies – including probably yours – have multiple cloud vendors. "Multi-cloud" is a trend that's growing partly because it's hard to find everything you want from one vendor and partly because companies like to hedge their bets in case things go wrong with their primary cloud provider(s). Some companies believe that multi-cloud computing is inevitable because cloud providers specialize in some capabilities but not others. But as I argue below, be careful how wide you cast your cloud net. The more cloud vendors you use, the more service level agreements (SLAs) you must manage and the more money you will spend.

Note also that there are three kinds of clouds: public, private and hybrid. As their names suggest, the distinction is about security, privacy and protection. Public cloud computing enables most SaaS, IaaS and PaaS activity. Private cloud computing enables companies to protect their data and applications with a "firewall" that shields the company from public access in the classic "multi-tenant" public cloud computing model. It's a security play for sure, especially for companies that design and develop lots of applications, or companies that want customized infrastructures. Many companies use "hybrid clouds" with elements of public and private cloud computing. Hybrid clouds enable companies to decide what's "private" and what's "public."

Cloud computing decisions require some matrix thinking. There are three primary cloud computing offerings – IaaS, PaaS and SaaS – and three ways to access the cloud – public, private and hybrid cloud computing. These capabilities and access methods may be complicated by the number of cloud vendors your hire. The 3:3 matrix may actually occur across cloud vendors, especially if you insist upon living in complicated cloud worlds.

Why should you care?

If your cloud environment is a "bit of this and a bit of that", you're already in trouble. Let me explain. Your goal is simplicity. If you spend most of your time untangling your cloud mess or negotiating cloud service level agreements (SLAs) across multiple vendors, you're missing opportunities to leverage cloud for competitive advantage. Remember, you have no choice but to care a lot about cloud computing. It's the way you offer products and services to your clients and the way you access products and services from your vendors. You cannot run your business without a major commitment to cloud computing since many of the applications you use will be available only in the cloud and many of the products and services you sell will be sold only from the cloud. Many of the emerging technology platforms you need are also hosted in the cloud. You must also care because cloud computing – when done right – is cost-effective. It shifts cash from fixed to variable spending, from CAPEX to OPEX (from capital expenditures to operational expenditures [Ross, 2022], which for lots of reasons is preferable to CAPEX. None of this is debatable – because it's inevitable).

What should you do about it?

Here's where it gets challenging – especially with the cacophony of marketing hype in your head. There are very few questions left about the comprehensiveness of cloud services: it's already huge – and it's growing. Short-term and easily long-term, on-premise computing is dead. Stop listening to the naysayers and critics who believe we'll return to in-house data centres. Cloud business cases have long since been validated and it won't be long until just about all applications and data are hosted in someone's cloud. Emerging technologies are now part of the cloud providers' repertoire. *Amazon*, for example, offers tools in analytics, augmented reality, virtual reality, the Internet of Things (IoT), blockchain, robotics and machine learning. *IBM* offers capabilities in artificial intelligence, the Internet of Things, blockchain and analytics. *Google* offers capabilities in analytics, artificial intelligence and the Internet of Things. *Microsoft* offers tools in artificial intelligence, machine learning, blockchain, IoT and analytics. They're all pretty much offering the same technologies-as-a-service. They're operational commodities *and* strategic differentiators. Use them.

But there's another cloud trend you must track: consolidation. At the time of this writing, four vendors own close to 75 per cent of the cloud infrastructure market. Three providers – *Amazon* Web Services, *Microsoft* and *Google* – own over 50 per cent of the overall cloud market. This kind of market concentration is – as always – good and bad – for all of the obvious reasons. But concentration also assumes the need to select a major cloud partner (among a shrinking set) as soon as possible in order to optimise their products and services. Since the largest cloud providers have the deepest product/service catalogues, you have no choice but to select from among a handful of providers. While companies benefit tremendously from soup-to-nuts provisioning, they're at risk if the number of providers shrinks.

The combination of full-provisioning and cloud oligarchy equals total dependency. While the trend toward richer cloud products and services is terrific, the availability of the products and services from a shrinking number of providers is not. Proceed with caution. Pick one of the oligarchs, make your best deal, and manage performance closely – you don't have a choice.

There's another reason why cloud management is a new, in-house core competency. Do not hire a consultant to manage your cloud consultants. If you do this, you'll be two arms' lengths away from control of perhaps your overall most important technology delivery asset. If you haven't already done so, you should determine your internal and external cloud computing requirements. While you need most things cloud, which ones? PaaS, IaaS, SaaS, others as a service? How much? How many? How scalable? What should you pay?

Again, how you manage all this is an internal core competency. This is a relatively new skill. It's also one that requires brains – your brains – not the brains of what has emerged as yet another consulting industry around "cloud management". This is one of the examples of where in-house brains should trump outside "brains". Your brain needs to focus on requirements, cloud management, migration plans and container technology (DeMuro, 2019) to make it easier to move your data and applications from one cloud provider to another if that becomes necessary). Containers are table stakes. But the real challenges include how you decide upon providers, the number of providers you need, the kind of services you require (IaaS, SaaS, PaaS, etc.) and how hybrid and private you want to be. *The unequivocal advice here is to have as few cloud providers as possible, as little hybrid services as possible and private provisioning only when it's absolutely necessary. The advice also includes relying on your cloud provider(s) to provide emerging technology services.* Finally, you need to focus your efforts on cloud-native applications and services, which means you need to build applications that exploit the cloud's natural distributed computing capabilities that scale flexibly in the cloud.

Cloud is unquestionably the future of your applications – built with low-code platforms (Raju, 2021). (See how all this fits together?) Your team must understand the range of cloud solutions, container technology, the emerging technology capabilities of cloud providers, cloud management, cloud relationship management and cloud performance metrics – all as summarised in cloud plays.

CLOUD COMPUTING PLAYS

Without cloud providers, you have no business. This kind of dependency is unprecedented. So, proceed with every ounce of due diligence you can find.

Your cloud providers own your internal business processes and the hosting of the products and services you provide others. As such, it deserves an extraordinary amount of attention which must come from inside your company: do not cede control over your cloud decision making to external consultants. Cloud management is a clear and obvious core competency. The specific steps for cloud effectiveness you should take include:

- *Conduct an ongoing cloud requirement analysis resulting in the allocation of cloud investments in IaaS, PaaS, SaaS and other capabilities as a service.*
- *Invest in container technology.*
- *Seek as few cloud providers as possible.*
- *Resist hybrid cloud architectures.*
- *Pilot emerging technologies platformed in the cloud.*
- *Shift development to cloud-native applications with low-code platforms.*
- *Track cloud technology trends, especially consolidation trends which may limit your choices; and, while it's difficult to escape oligarchs, you should always have a contingency plan.*
- *Above all else, develop a world-class internal cloud management team capable of negotiating and tracking cloud contracts.*

CYBERSECURITY MESH

The number of cyberattacks will grow. The *SolarWinds* debacle was a warm-up (Jibilian and Canales, 2021). Anyone who tells you that cyber-security is working or even adequate is lying. The computing industry – despite all its wonder – is vulnerable to a wide variety of attacks.

Will a "mesh" help?

What is it?

The Gartner Group defines cybersecurity mesh as (Gartner, 2022a):

> *"Cybersecurity mesh is a flexible, composable architecture that integrates widely distributed and disparate security services. Cyber-security mesh enables best-of-breed, stand-alone security solutions to work together to improve overall security while moving control points closer to the assets they're designed to protect. It can quickly and reliably verify identity, context and policy adherence across cloud and non-cloud environments."*

Here's a working definition:

> *A cybersecurity "mesh" is a multi-level network of connections that secures multiple devices each with their own security defenses. Unlike more traditional approaches to cybersecurity, a mesh is far more effective than one-to-one security, especially across cloud computing infrastructure and applications.*

Why should you care?

These definitions point the way to problems and solutions. Note that there's an entire chapter in this book – Chapter 5 – about why you should worry a lot and invest even more in cybersecurity. We'll discuss the range of personal and professional threats, obligatory and quasi-effective cybersecurity and some of the methods, tools, platforms and partners you need to survive what is – and will continue to be – endless attacks on your digital life. Suffice it to say here, you have no choice but to care a lot about cybersecurity.

Note also that cybersecurity technology is both operational and stra-tegic. If your operational infrastructure is vulnerable, you cannot practise strategic differentiation.

What should you do about it?

Chapter 5 outlines the steps. As they say: *"Wait for it".*

APPLICATIONS TECHNOLOGIES

Let's turn now to the technologies that enable the development of applications.

SOCIAL MEDIA ANALYTICS (SMA)

What is it?

(Qualtrics^{XM}, 2022; the **bold** is mine):

> *"Social media analytics* **. . . includes tracking conversations and measuring campaigns. It also involves figuring out how your social activities are influencing your business results** *. . . for some people social media analytics is focused on the operational metrics associated with their social media channels. For campaigns and strategies run through social media, it's common that marketing professionals will analyze their social media metrics – focusing on conversion rates, follower counts, and impressions."*

Why should you care?

> *"***Proven ROI for your brand strategy***: analyzing all social media data – plus add-ons like review monitoring or digital customer care data – helps you understand your customers' needs and preferences so you can build an effective brand strategy . . .* **make more strategic business decisions***: you can see clearer paths to success when you've got in-depth analysis of how your customers view your brand and interact with your platforms."*

What should you do about it?

SMA methods, tools and platforms are evolving all the time. They're close to full automation – which is where AI and machine learning meets social media analytics. This is the trend that's important – a trend you should know more about. What if you could direct the technology – not your human team – to track and describe, explain, predict and prescribe all things social?

Augmented analytics is the broader trend you must track. Augmented analytics marries traditional analytics with AI and machine learning where machine learning enables the data selection and preparation processes with algorithms trained to expedite key analytics steps.

SMA is where analytics gets smart. What to do? It's a two-step process. Step one is the piloting of social media analytics platforms, such as *Sprout*, *HubSpot* and *Google* Analytics (Barnhart, 2021). Step two is a pilot in augmented analytics like what *IBM* and *Microsoft* Power BI enable. The outcome of all this are dashboards that report 24/7 on any and all devices you authorise.

Before I forget, there's a step you should never take. Unless politics is your business, never, ever, go there. Do not blog, tweet, post or partake in social or political "causes". It never ends well. Elon Musk's *Twitter* debacle is a perfect example of how social media can backfire on your ultimate goals, which in Musk's case is to sell as many cars as he can and pioneer space travel, among other activities. Stay away from politics – no matter how seductive it might be.

WEARABLES

What are they?

Wearables are what they do – devices that collect and interpret data in real-time usually from direct contact with someone's body (or through indirect contact, such as through sensors embedded in clothes or football helmets). These devices use sensors to collect data and algorithms to interpret the "signals" which can stand-alone or be transmitted over the Internet where additional interpreters can further assess the collected data. Wearables and the Internet of Things (IoT) are close cousins, if not brothers and sisters. They work closely together to collect and interpret all kinds of data. Healthcare is adopting wearables quickly where remote monitoring is becoming a low-cost way to check on the health of patients.

You've seen them; they might even be working closely with – or embedded in/on – you (smart watches, pacemakers, fitness trackers, GPS trackers, etc.).

Why should you care?

As with many of these technologies, relevance depends upon your industry or your plans to enter adjacent or whole new industries with your products and services. Applications here are everywhere across many industries, especially healthcare, fitness and entertainment, and all industries where sensors collect and transmit data with Bluetooth, WiFi and GPS. If you're in these businesses, you should care a lot about how you – and your competitors – use wearable technology to enhance your processes, products and services.

What should you do about them?

If you're in an industry where wearables are obvious, you should already be piloting hardware, software or networking applications – or all three. There's a growing market for wearables. The key is to anticipate where and how wearable technology will impact your business. *Be generous with your relevance assessment.* There are so many applications across so many industries that there may be more applications than you initially believe. Think about it this way. If you're in the clothing, eye, entertainment, healthcare, education, training, supply chain, logistics, athletic, automotive, shoe, construction or ear business, well, you get the point. Wearable technology has massive potential across many industries. Just because applications don't immediately jump into your lap, doesn't mean they're not there. "Mine" your processes, products and services with an expansive eye across the next three–five years regarding the impact wearables might have on your business. Once the door opens, explore partnerships, markets and, as always, what your competitors are doing.

Finally, don't forget the value of the data that wearable devices collect. This data can be as valuable as the wearable product or service you're selling and, in some cases, much more valuable. Subject to privacy regulations, this data can be sold over and over again to a variety of companies that need continuous insight into their customers and customer behaviour. The monetisation of wearable data can become a significant revenue stream.

AUGMENTED AND VIRTUAL REALITY

What are they?

Augmented and virtual reality technology are growing as more and more major technology players join the trend. *Apple*, for example, has entered the headset race (Seeking Alpha, 2021). *Microsoft* is selling massive deals to the *US* military (Sag, 2021). The gaming industry is fully committed (Fortune Business Insights, 2021), and there's no metaverse without AR/VR (Levy, 2021). This is another technology that needs some depth.

> *"Augmented reality (AR) is an interactive experience of a real-world habitat where aspects of the real world are enhanced by computer-generated information. AR is a system that brings together three features: a merging of real and virtual environments, real-time interaction, and accurate three-dimensional registration of both virtual and real things. AR changes a person's perception of the real world, whereas virtual reality completely replaces the real world with an artificial one."*

"Virtual reality (VR) is a simulated experience that can be either the same as or totally different from the real world. Uses of VR include entertainment (particularly gaming), education (for example, in medical or military training) and business (for meeting virtually). At present, standard VR uses either a head set or multi-projected environments to achieve realistic images, noises and other impressions that replicate the user's physical existence in the virtual environment."

Why should you care?

Like many of the technologies discussed here, AR and VR technology have enormous potential – even in industries you don't immediately associate with AR and VR, including perhaps yours. Your due diligence should focus on the business processes, modelling and mining that will enable you to decide if AR and VR merit pilots.

What should you do about them?

If you're in the education, travel, entertainment, gaming and healthcare industries, you should designate a special team to dig deep into the potential of AR and VR technology. Pilot applications and build financial models around products and services enabled by AR and VR. If you haven't already done this, track how your competition is using the technologies. One last thing: track the hardware players as closely as the software players. When *Apple* enters the headset market, it will change everyone's plans for AR/VR. Your due diligence should shadow theirs.

ROBOTICS

What is it?

(Britannica, 2022)

*"**Robotics** is the imagining, building, and usage of machines created to carry out tasks that have traditionally been done by humans. Robots are used in industries such as car manufacturing to carry out straightforward, repetitive tasks, and in industries where environments can be hazardous to human beings. Many facets of robotics involve artificial intelligence (AI); robots may have the equivalent of human senses such as sight, touch, and the ability to recognise temperature."*

Read this too:

"Robotics creates machines that can replace humans and duplicate human actions. Robots can be used in a variety of situations for many different purposes, but presently many are used in hazardous situations (for example, in testing radioactive materials or detecting and deactivating explosives), in manufacturing processes, or in situations where humans would not survive (e.g., in space, under water, in extreme heat, or in the management or clean-up of dangerous materials)."

Got it? It's impossible to ignore the impact "robots" will have.

Why should you care?

Simple: robots are much more efficient than humans for huge classes of tasks. If you ignore this opportunity, you will lose market share.

What should you do about it?

Survey your existing products and services for robotic opportunities. Then imagine your next generation products and services enabled by robotics. Another Tiger Team? Yes. Another COE? No – unless your business processes will be directly affected – that's disintermediated – by robotics.

IoT/IoE

What are they?

The Internet of Things (IoT) and the Internet of Everything (IoE) are macro trends that enable and blend with other technology trends. IoE represents connectivity at the highest level of analysis, where data is collected across processes and functions within and beyond specific business models. IoE is the overarching activity that enables the Internet of Things, a subset of IoE. Think about IoE as a sports league comprised a specific teams where specific activities (IoT games) occur. Both are networks of devices that collect and interpret data, information and knowledge over wireless networks like the Internet and supporting networks. IoT enables all sorts of analytical activities. Some of these activities are enabled by machine intelligence where the collection and analysis of data is partially or fully automated. Some is more traditional. As suggested, IoT works seamlessly with wearables.

Connectivity is the watchword here.
But it's also about the business processes enabled by connectivity.

Why should you care?

Anything you have that's already connected or that should be connected is why you should care.

What should you do about them?

Take stock of your processes, products and services. Where are the opportunities? What are the costs? Are there security risks? What's the competition doing with IoT/IoE? Where appropriate, prototype.

AI AND MACHINE LEARNING

What is it?

Artificial intelligence (AI) and machine learning (ML) are members of perhaps the most exciting and important business-technology field of the last several decades. The applications of AI/ML to business models and processes are endless. AI/ML focus on the automation of business processes and tasks, intelligent decision making, predictive analytics, personalisation and conversational interfaces, among many other areas. The elements of AI include machine learning, natural language processing, algorithms, computer vision, image recognition and robotics. There is "narrow" AI/ML and "generalised" AI/ML which refers to the "boundability" of the problem. Most problems are well-bounded problems, that is, problems that can be modelled. For example, automating the process by which someone should receive a loan, or whether someone should be admitted to a university, can be modelled quite easily, since the variables that predict to accept/reject are known and can be labelled. Algorithms can be developed that "predict" to acceptance/rejection in these cases straightforwardly. Natural language understanding and generation include the ability to understand written and spoken language to create dialogue that solves problems, like customer service interaction. Computer vision and image recognition power autonomous vehicles.

Why should you care?

AI and machine learning can literally change your business processes and possibly your entire business model. The venture community believes this, countless corporate venture capitalists know it and entrepreneurs are gathering at the gates of every industry on the planet. Why? Intelligent systems save money and make money. Remember the only two metrics that matter? AI and machine learning have that kind of potential. Am I overstating this? Probably. But the premise is sound. You have no choice but to care a lot about AI and machine learning.

What should you do about it?

Chapter 4 is devoted to AI and machine learning. It discusses how to develop the right applications, how to select the best platforms and partner and, maybe – just maybe – launch a Centre of Excellence. In-house, of course.

3D MODELLING AND MANUFACTURING

What are they?

First, they're impressive. Much more impressive than the metaverse, at least at this point in time. Here's what 3D modelling is all about (Take Off Professionals (TOPS), 2022):

> *"The term '3D modeling' refers to the process of creating a three-dimensional representation of an object using specialized software. This representation, called a 3D model, can convey an object's size, shape and texture. You can create 3D models of existing items, as well as designs that have not yet been built in real life."*

What about 3D *manufacturing*? Here's an understanding (GE, 2022; the **bold** is mine):

> *"Additive manufacturing (AM), also known as 3D printing, is **a transformative approach to industrial production that enables the creation of lighter, stronger parts and systems.***
>
> *"**Additive manufacturing uses computer-aided-design (CAD) software or 3D object scanners to direct hardware to deposit material, layer upon layer, in precise geometric shapes** . . . additive manufacturing adds material to create an object . . . in the right applications, additive manufacturing delivers a perfect trifecta of improved performance, complex geometries and simplified fabrication. As a result, opportunities abound for those who actively embrace additive manufacturing."*

Why should you care?

Porsche is prototyping pistons with additive manufacturing (Aysha M., 2020). Additive manufacturers are also building houses and bridges. Market size (CMTC, 2021; the **bold** is mine)?

> *"The global additive manufacturing market size is projected to be sized at $30.6 billion in 2028. Other reports estimate the market to grow by a high rate of 14.4% a year. It's expected that manufacturing will garner nearly 33% of the total market share by 2027 . . . the driving force behind this rapid growth is the ability of additive manufacturing technologies for companies* **to shift from prototyping applications to efficient mass production of parts, components, and accessories.***"*

What should you do about them?

Look closely at your products. Where are they manufactured? What are the components? Is there an additive manufacturing pilot that makes sense? If it's good for *Porsche*, it's good for you. Prototype.

TOTAL EXPERIENCE (TX)

Everyone talks a good game about digital "experience". Everyone wants to make the experience of their employees and customers as pleasant and productive as possible. The fact is that digital experiences are still largely horrific for "users". No? Have you ever "chatted" with a bot? Have you ever waited for a customer service representative? Have you ever waited for a response to a question you posed? TX is an aspiration, not yet even remotely close to a reality.

What is it (Morrow, 2021)?

> *"Total experience is based on the idea that no experience operates in a vacuum. Employee experience impacts customer experience. User experience impacts employee experience, and so on . . . they are interconnected and interdependent, and yet because of how they evolved as business disciplines, they are rarely treated as such. More often than not, companies have teams and software solutions dedicated to a particular experience (customer experience, user experience, etc.), and those teams and solutions run independently of one another."*

Let's expand this a little (Humanperf Blog, 2021):

> *"Total Experience (TX) is therefore a blend not only of CX, EX and OX, but also some new abbreviations for other concepts to be adopted, e.g., PX for Partner Experience, SX for Supplier Experience, and so on.*
>
> *"Yet it is not so much a matter of concepts and abbreviations as meaning, i.e. the meaning that is given to everyone's activities. We are definitely talking here about the business' development strategy."*

TX is where user experience (UX) meets employee experience (EX) meets operational experience (OX) and any other "X" that can be integrated wholistically into the "experience".

Why should you care?

A lot of the competition in the all-digital world will be in the "experience" area. It's that simple. If you're competing in an all-digital world – which you are – you must care about digital experience. In spite of whatever scepticism you might have about the integration of all of the "Xs", you have no choice but to invest in TX.

What should you do about it?

First, develop a TX strategy, which is easily a brains activity. Find the vendors – the brawn – that offer TX platforms. While many of these vendors are still selling older experiences, they're also moving as quickly as they can to the TX world. You need a team to call the shots here and some strong partners that understand the migration path from CX, EX, etc. to TX. You also need to listen to your customers, clients and users when they complain about access, transaction processing and problem resolution. If you're a little sceptical of the complaints, become a customer for a week. Try your products and services. Sit in a service queue. Stay on hold for an hour. You get the idea.

THE METAVERSE

What is it?

If you really want to understand the metaverse, start with Second Life which, by the way, was founded in 2003 (Wikpeida, 2022).

> *"Second Life is a multimedia web platform where people can create a personal avatar and have a second life in a virtual world. Second Life is similar to multi-player online role-playing games; however, Linden*

Lab is clear that their creation is not a game: 'there is no manufac-tured conflict, no set objective.'"

"Second Life users (or "residents") create virtual alternative versions of themselves ("avatars"), and interact with places, things and other avatars. They can explore the world (the "grid"), mingle with other residents, take part in individual and group activities, go shopping, take part in the trade of virtual property, build, create and trade virtual services with others.""

The metaverse, like *Second Life,* is a digital world in which all kinds of activities take place. You can conduct meetings, buy things, have fun and even "live" in the virtual real estate you buy – maybe even next door to Snoop Dogg (Melnick, 2021; if you have a spare $450,000 lying around). Here's another description (Welsh, 2022):

"These three elements – a VR interface, digital ownership, and avatars – still feature prominently in current conceptions of the metaverse. But none of them is actually essential to the idea. In the broadest terms, the metaverse is understood as a graphically rich virtual space, with some degree of verisimilitude, where people can work, play, shop, socialize – in short, do the things humans like to do together in real life (or, perhaps more to the point, on the internet). Metaverse proponents often focus on the concept of "presence" *as a defining factor: feeling like you're really there and feeling like other people are really there with you, too.*

"This version of the metaverse arguably already exists in the form of video games. But there's another definition of the metaverse that goes beyond the virtual worlds we know. This definition doesn't actually describe the metaverse at all but does explain why everyone thinks it's so important."

Why should you care?

This is a complex question because of the short-term and longer-term impli-cations of a new interactive digital world – a new internet. Pieces of this world are already in place through the technologies that will enable a larger digital experience, like augmented and virtual reality. Short term, you should care if you're part of the infrastructure that will enable the metaverse or plan to sell non-fungible token (NFT) digital products and services there. Longer term, there's room there for all kinds of revenue streams – so long as you define "longer term".

What should you do about it?

First, determine where you sit – or want to sit – in the metaverse ecosystem. Do you make the chips that will power the devices in the metaverse? Do you develop applications that will enable transactions in the metaverse? Companies like *Nvidia*, *Unity* and *Roblox*, for example, have clear roles to play. If you're in any of the main elements of the metaverse, like immersive hardware (headsets and beyond), 3D hardware and software, interactivity, connectivity, semiconductors and especially cybersecurity, then there's a play. If you're a total solutions provider, you need to partner with metaverse infrastructure providers. But if your products and services are far removed from the metaverse, then you have more time. Even if there's no relationship between your *current* products and services, there well may be in the not-too-distant future and more likely in the longer term, especially for adjacent and whole products and services – so watch this space carefully. For example, there are many businesses not currently thinking about the metaverse as a revenue stream that should at least start exploring possibilities. The *Wealth Quint Team* lists some possibilities (2022) such as virtual events, immersing learning, immersive shopping, gaming, advertising, education and virtual travel, among other areas.

PROCESS/TECHNOLOGY MATCHES – PROTOTYPING

This list of technologies is deliberately long. You must track them all – and more. You need a team of in-house professionals – full-time employees – to identify and track the technologies most likely to impact your business. The list changes all the time, mostly through additions, seldom subtractions, but don't outsource this. This is a core competency.

The list of business processes and sub-processes can also be long. Without lists of technologies and business processes, matching (and subsequent prototyping) is impossible. Both lists must be developed and vetted on a continuing basis.

You also need some discipline around the technology assessment process designed to vet technology impact upon current and future business models and processes and answer two simple questions: *"Will this technology help us make money, save money, or both?"* and *"What processes will it improve, automate, eliminate or reinvent?"*

Remember that technology assessments follow their own protocols, their own repeatable steps. This is a formal, funded process, not something assigned to a few people when the mood strikes. The assessment process should also include a competitive analysis targeted at knowing how your competitors are assessing and investing in emerging digital technologies.

Now look at Figures 8 and 9. Figure 8 describes two steps to leverage technology. Step one is how most of us think about technology leverage. We look for opportunities to improve, automate or even eliminate *existing* processes, products and services with new technologies. But step two is very different. Here we look for opportunities to use technologies to inspire all *new* processes, products and services. Step one is more about incremental changes; step two is disruptive. Figure 9 describes the relationship between processes and technologies. Note that this too is a two-way arrangement, where the processes link to as-is and to-be processes and vice versa.

How do *you* think about leverage?

Here are some ideas. First, identify the processes that take the most time, cost you the most money and are the most amenable to technology disruption (or at least change). (You should already have this list via your process mining activities.) Figure 9, for example, models the loan acceptance/rejection process. Which of the sub-processes could be improved, automated, eliminated or completely reimagined? Which technologies "match" with each of the improve/automate/eliminate or completely reimagine objectives? How might the processes and sub-processes around loans be improved, automated, eliminated or completely reimagined? Which technologies could yield such outcomes? It's the same for the lender and the loan officer: which technologies could improve, automate, eliminate or completely reimagine the loan acceptance/rejection processes and sub-processes?

Hypotheses can be generated, such as "machine learning can automate huge chunks of the loan assessment process" and "natural language processing can assist the evaluation process." Can these "matches" be tested? Sure, via prototyping.

The prototyping process should be standardised, like the business case templates everyone's expected to use. Prototyping has seven steps:

1. Describe the emerging technology with reference to business impact.
2. Specify impact hypotheses about the impact on specific business models and processes.
3. Identify sponsors (and resources) to champion demonstration prototypes.
4. Develop prototyping project plans (with empirical impact metrics).
5. Standardise prototyping methods, tools and techniques.
6. Develop the prototypes, consisting of process descriptions and computer-based demonstrations.
7. Assess the impact of the prototype demonstrations on the way to further testing, as suggested by Figure 10.

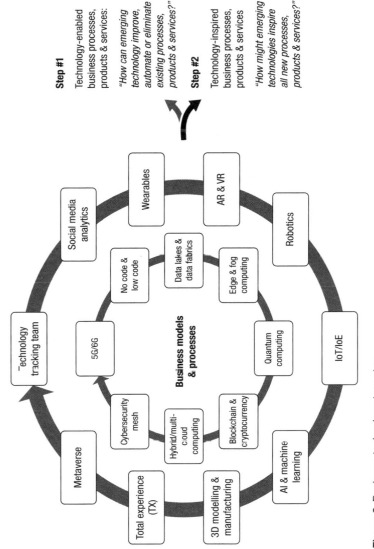

Step #1

Technology-enabled business processes, products & services:

"How can emerging technology improve, automate or eliminate existing processes, products & services?"

Step #2

Technology-inspired business processes, products & services

"How might emerging technologies inspire all new processes, products & services?"

Wearables

AR & VR

Robotics

Social media analytics

No code & low code

Data lakes & data fabrics

Edge & fog computing

IoT/IoE

Technology tracking team

5G/6G

Business models & processes

Quantum computing

Cybersecurity mesh

Hybrid/multi-cloud computing

Blockchain & cryptocurrency

AI & machine learning

Metaverse

Total experience (TX)

3D modelling & manufacturing

Figure 8 Business-technology two-step

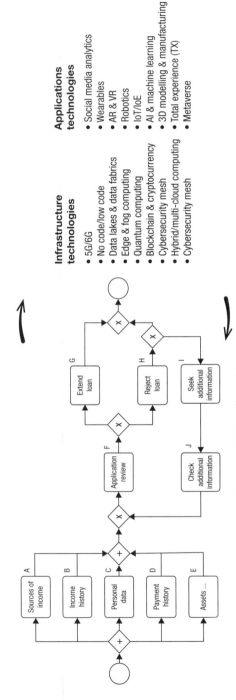

Infrastructure technologies

- 5G/6G
- No code/low code
- Data lakes & data fabrics
- Edge & fog computing
- Quantum computing
- Blockchain & cryptocurrency
- Cybersecurity mesh
- Hybrid/multi-cloud computing
- Cybersecurity mesh

Applications technologies

- Social media analytics
- Wearables
- AR & VR
- Robotics
- IoT/IoE
- AI & machine learning
- 3D modelling & manufacturing
- Total experience (TX)
- Metaverse

Figure 9 Emerging technologies for disruptive digital transformation

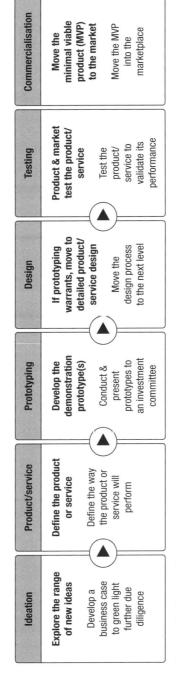

Figure 10 Stage-gating

Matching and prototyping are two plays that will help you win.

They're the "go-to" plays you should execute all the time. Perhaps now you understand why I'm so dogmatic about core competencies. Leverage comes from a deep understanding of business processes and a wide understanding of existing and emerging digital technology. No one can understand your business better than your team. Your team must also understand technology to identify the most potentially impactful process/technology matches. Outsourcing the matching process to consultants is a mistake. If you don't have a team that can match processes and technologies, build one. But don't default to consultants who have half-baked ideas about how your industry works, where it's going, who you are, what you do and what you need to succeed. Can you really tell me they can – *or should* – do all this better than you?

Does all this make sense? It sure better.

Much like exercising to stay healthy, the process described here is absolutely achievable. Why it seldom occurs is a question for students of human nature. *But I can tell you without question that if you model processes, track technologies, match process/technology opportunities and prototype the potential, you will win the strategic technology game. I can also tell you that all this can be done inside your company's (physical or virtual) walls.*

TRACKING, MATCHING AND PROTOTYPING PLAYS

Tracking digital technology is an in-house core competency.

The essence of tracking is about features, not bits and bytes. Does the technology make things faster, secure and easier to experience? Does it make applications more accessible – and "adjustable"? Does it automate more processes with relative ease? Do cloud vendors support the technologies? Are they cheaper to deploy? Do they scale? These are the questions that reveal their features, their abilities and likely cost-effectiveness. These are the questions executives, managers and directors should be asking:

- *What is it?*
- *Why should you care?*
- *What should you do about it?*

As-is and to-be processes are matched with the most promising enabling existing and emerging technologies – which is a brains activity. Prototyping follows matching. Stage-gating can help assess prototypes.

CHAPTER 3

KEEP DIGITAL TRANSFORMATION IN PERSPECTIVE

CHAPTER SUMMARY

- *There are many types of digital transformation; make sure you select the type that "works" for your company.*
- *There are digital transformation "myths" you must dispel.*
- *There are requirements that must be satisfied for successful digital transformation.*
- *There are specific steps you should take to implement a digital transformation project.*
- *There's a "soft side" to digital transformation you cannot ignore.*

DIGITAL TRANSFORMATION

Digital transformation comes in all shapes and sizes. Most "digital transformation" projects, however, are not "transformative". They don't *disrupt* business processes or whole business models – you already know this. Instead, they're "incremental" or just as often part of planned technology "modernisation" initiatives. These kinds of projects are safer, less expensive and "politically" protective of executive reputations, which is perhaps why most digital transformation projects focus on incremental changes or modernisation. But real digital transformation projects are truly transformative, targeted at replacing or automating business processes, or replacing or automating whole business models – which – again – are riskier, more expensive and politically dangerous than incremental/modernisation ones.

Impact and risk are brothers and sisters: incremental/modernisation projects are easily less impactful than disruptive ones. You need to decide what and how you want to "transform", acknowledging the likely return on your digital transformation investments. But eventually, because of the trajectories of technology and business, you will have to pursue more disruptive transformation and leave incremental transformation to operational technologists.

What *is* digital transformation?

According to *Salesforce.com* (2022), digital transformation (the **bold** is mine):

> *" . . . is the process of using digital technologies **to create new – or modify existing – business processes,** culture, and customer experiences to meet changing business and market requirements. **This reimagining of business in the digital age is digital transformation."***

The Enterprisers Project offers yet another definition (The Enterprises Project, 2016; the **bold** is mine):

> *"Digital transformation is the **integration of digital technology into all areas of a business, fundamentally changing how you operate and deliver value to customers.** It's also a cultural change that requires organizations to continually challenge the status quo, experiment, and get comfortable with failure."*

SAS (2022) describes it this way (the **bold** is mine):

> *"Digital transformation refers to the process and strategy of **using digital technology to drastically change how businesses operate and serve customers.**"*

ZDNet sees it this way (Samuels, 2021; the **bold** is mine):

> *"Digital transformation involves **using digital technologies to remake a process to become more efficient or effective.** The idea is to use technology not just to replicate an existing service in a digital form, but to use technology to transform that service into something significantly better . . . digital transformation can involve many different technologies, but the hottest topics right now are cloud computing, the Internet of Things, big data, and artificial intelligence."*

Let's just stipulate that digital transformation includes activities that include a wide range of activities ranging from upgrading existing systems, replacing legacy systems, developing digital applications that modify existing processes, and completely reinventing business processes that barely resemble existing processes and even whole business models – which is what everyone describes as disruptive transformation. Just remember – as discussed throughout the book – that there's always a risk/reward calculation at work. The more disruptive, the riskier the transformation project is. If you want to play it safe, tell everyone that your system upgrade project is actually real digital transformation. Everyone does it, so don't feel embarrassed when you announce your ambitious digital transformation project to improve the interface of your twenty-year old application.

Definitions vary according to the emphasis placed on business processes versus whole business models, or incremental versus disruptive transformation. (Which is your favourite?) As described, most digital transformation projects – despite their aspirations – are incremental or part of planned technology modernisation efforts, as described in Figure 11.

Where are you in this matrix? What have you been "selling" as digital transformation?

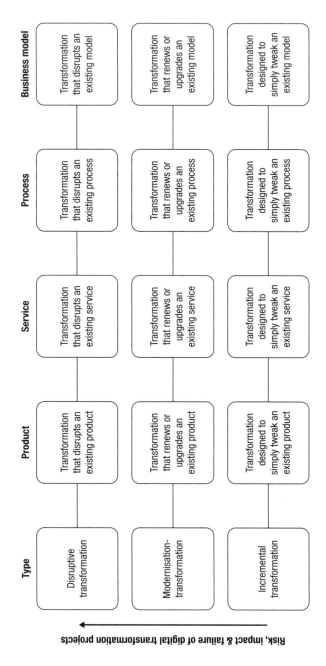

Figure 11 The type, impact and risks of digital transformation projects

Figure 11 suggests that incremental and modernisation projects are by definition "safer" than ones targeted at disrupting business processes and models. But incremental DT projects also have limited impact on a company's strategic mission. The trade-off is straightforward: stay with safer, simpler projects – or attempt to disrupt business processes and whole business models through riskier DT projects. As the figure suggests, the further one moves across the DT continuum, the greater the impact. So, while the impact of incremental projects is relatively small, so are the risks.

The difference between incremental/modernisation transformation is small and, in fact, not that different from business as usual. Will incremental/modernisation DT keep companies competitive? Will it enable profitable growth? Is it responsive to the competition? Can companies respond slowly to market trends believing they always have time to pivot to more disruptive behaviour? Or should they pivot to disruptive transformation? You know the answer to all these questions.

The promise of disruptive digital transformation lies far from incremental or modernisation projects. Real transformation can transform business processes and whole business models if certain things are true. Can we just call it strategic transformation?

DISPEL DIGITAL TRANSFORMATION MYTHS

There are myths surrounding digital transformation. I reported on five of them in the past (Andriole, 2017). Let's revisit them with some "perspective" gained after some time studying the promise and perils of digital transformation.

Myth #1: Some companies can skip digital transformation

Every company must obviously incrementally change the way it does business and modernise its aging systems. Companies that refuse to change at all will find themselves at a competitive disadvantage. So, yes, every company needs to digitally transform, but we should note that refusals to change at all will likely be listed by the business coroner as the most likely cause of death.

Myth #2: Digital transformation leverages emerging or disruptive technologies

Incremental and modernisation-focused DT often use conventional, existing digital technology. There's often no need to adopt *emerging* technology to affect incremental changes or modernisation projects – so this myth still stands. Incremental/modernisation DT can stick with tried-and-true technologies (until they can't). But *disruptive transformation* almost always leverages emerging technology. Technology's role is obvious.

Myth #3: Profitable companies are most likely to launch digital transformation projects

The assumption that market leaders are the most innovative is usually false (Christensen, 1997). Companies doing well often believe that doing well is the result of repetitive processes and an unassailable business model. They do not always believe their path to profitability should be disrupted. This is still true.

Myth #4: You need to disrupt your industry before someone else does

Market leaders do not usually sense disruptive competition, especially from new entrants. So, no, market leaders are not obsessed with vulnerability. Instead, they feel strong and powerful, even invulnerable to disruptors that impact whole industries, like *Airbnb* (hospitality), *Uber* and *Lyft* (transportation), *Amazon* (retail), *SelectQuote* (insurance) and *Netflix* (entertainment), among others that have reinvented a broad range of vertical industries.

Myth #5: Executives are hungry for digital transformation

They're still not – unless their companies (and therefore themselves) are threatened by falling revenues and serious competition. But that doesn't stop executives from talking endlessly about their digital transformation projects and goals (Andriole, 2017):

> *"There's a widening gap between what executives say about digital transformation and what they actually do. It would be nice to think that executives are primarily motivated by what's best for the long-term health of the company, but their motives are often more complex."*

These myths mostly speak to readiness.
How ready are you – really?

TRANSFORMATION REQUIREMENTS

Myths aside, *you must assess the environment in which transformation will occur.* Some verticals, for example, like financial services and healthcare, are more likely to transform their processes than others, like accounting. Vested interests – like saving money by reducing fraud with intelligent systems – are powerful drivers. You must be open to change and have the willingness to "sell" transformation for its business value: professional introverts need not apply. Nor should you be driven by panic. Support should also descend into business units (where resistance can be significant) by describing the business value of transformation at all levels, which should include the right incentives for the key players.

Second, *data must be plentiful and high-quality.* Not just piles of structured and unstructured corporate data (arranged in data lakes) about customers, production, manufacturing, distribution, competitors and processes, but high-quality data that's clean, consistent and analytically accessible. Transformation projects that involve big data analytics and artificial intelligence are especially dependent upon quality data. Sometimes, companies must be told that their current data repositories will not enable digital transformation. Understandably, these are tough conversations, but sometimes necessary before spending a ton of money on projects destined to fail: honesty and transparency are still keys to success.

Third, in addition to the right data and methodology, *digital transformation projects require additional capabilities that companies need to exhibit internally (brains) and externally (brawn).* The assumption is that companies – no matter how enthused they might be about digital transformation – cannot master all of the skills necessary to accomplish their goals. This is a significant acknowledgment and suggests that definitions of "core competency" cannot be satisfied internally by most – if not all – companies – yet. The brains around digital transformation – what to transform – are in-house brains. The brawn necessary to execute the projects can be found anywhere.

Fourth, *disruptive transformation is likely to be enabled by – and in many cases dependent upon – emerging digital technology.* Figure 12 lists the technologies that should be tracked. At the centre are the disruptive business processes and models that define the essence of transformation.

Figure 12 formalises the role that emerging technologies must play in disruptive digital transformation, including a team whose job it is to track emerging technologies and continuously assess their potential impact on disruptive transformation. Note that lists like these change all the time, so tracking emerging technologies is itself a discipline that needs talent, resources and milestones, especially as they all relate to macro trends such as *The Future of Work* and the *Fourth Industrial Revolution.*

Fifth – and most importantly – *disruptive digital transformation must challenge executives and corporate cultures sceptical of big projects designed to change existing business processes and, in some cases, whole business models.* As we know from project failures, data, talent, the lack of

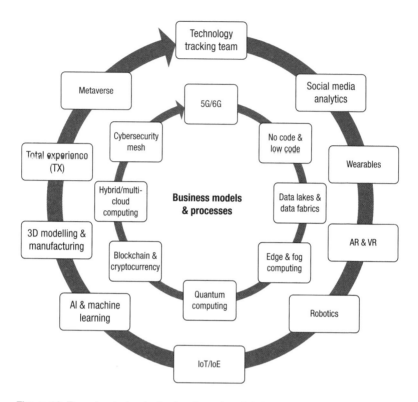

Figure 12 Emerging technologies for disruptive digital transformation

executive support and non-digital corporate cultures all contribute to project failure. Those committed to disruptive transformation cannot avoid these challenges. Objective assessments about industries, companies and the executives who run them are necessary for DT success.

You must decide about the type of digital transformation you want to pursue. Most decision-makers have already defaulted to incremental/ modernisation projects. They've decided that the risks of disruptive transformation are just too great, that the cost is too high and the political threats are too great. They also don't believe their industry (or competitors) has committed to disruptive change in any serious way, so they have time to play "catch-up". Relatively few decision-makers see digital transformation as an opportunity to disrupt business processes and business models to become market leaders. The ones who do are the courageous ones willing to take risks for profitable growth. I hope this describes you.

Example? AI and machine learning meets ERP.

Not so many years ago companies defined "digital transformation" as simply the application of digital technology to longstanding "normal" problems. Expectations were low. In most cases, digital transformation was like changing the oil with a new-and-improved oil filter. There was no talk of a newly designed engine. But more recently, companies have defined digital transformation much more ambitiously. Companies expect to modify, automate or replace processes with technology. They also expect to create brand new processes enabled by technology. While most "digital transformation" projects are still less than disruptive, the goal now is to improve, automate or replace some old processes that were previously time- or labour-intensive, and create new processes that can improve efficiency across multiple functional areas. The best digital transformation projects are ones that use emerging technology to solve old problems and automate new ones.

Companies rushed to standardise their business processes with enterprise resource planning (ERP) systems, like the formidable, almost pervasive, applications from SAP and other ERP vendors. The value proposition was – and remains – enterprise centralisation, standardisation and integration across internal and external business processes, cost savings and – in spite of their monolithic architectures – some flexibility (compared to the chaos that existed before). Kim O'Shaughnessy says it better (2016):

"Enterprise resource planning (ERP) systems are used by organizations looking to manage their business functions within a centralized and integrated system. ERP is commonly used by companies working within the supply chain to help keep track of all the moving parts of manufacturing and distribution. However, ERP can be utilized by a number of different industries including those in healthcare, nonprofit groups, construction and hospitality. Organizations needing to manage their staff, customers and inventory can all rely on ERP benefits . . . ERP stores all entered data into a single database, allowing all departments to work with the same information. Additionally, all this data can be organized, analyzed and made into reports. ERP brings together customer management, human resources, business intelligence, financial management, inventory and supply chain capabilities into one system."

For many companies, these operational capabilities were – and remain – a God-send. The basic functionality of enterprise applications can organise a company's business processes and whole business models. All good, for sure. But is this a sustainable role given what's happening with machine learning? Clearly, companies will invest heavily in automation to save money and eliminate, streamline and optimise processes. They will map and mine their business processes for maximum impact. They will do this as quickly as possible. The Covid-19 pandemic has obviously accelerated the drive toward automation. But the sprint to automation was well under way prior to the pandemic.

Digital transformation today is still about organisation and standardisation, but it's also about automation along a disruptive continuum. In fact, post-Covid-19, it will be much more about automation than functional standardisation. While enterprise applications vendors (like *SAP*) and ERP vendor enablers (like *UiPath*) are investing heavily in automation, the most automated companies will move past their enterprise applications to functionality that's increasingly automated outside of older application architectures. Why is this important? For one thing, post-Covid-19 companies will focus much more on the processes that can be automated than ones than can be "tracked" and "managed". Ideally, much of what enterprise application "users" do will be replaced by RPA and other intelligent bots. The obsession with "UI" and "UX" (user interfaces and user experiences), for example, will eventually vanish altogether.

How many companies will deploy new (or migrate from existing) ERP systems over the next ten years? Not as many as did ten years ago, that's for sure. Instead, they will:

1. Identify and model business problems.
2. Map and optimise business processes (via process mining; Davenport and Spanyi, 2019) that identify process optimisation opportunities.
3. Identify, collect, validate and leverage structured and unstructured data onto target business processes.
4. Match problems, processes, data and machine-learning algorithms.
5. Extend the approach to as many processes as possible.

These activities are all focused on automation. Said differently, they're focused on automating — and replacing — ERP modules and the processes like *"customer management, human resources, business intelligence, financial management, inventory and supply chain capabilities"* (O'Shaughnessy, 2016).

In fact, much of the internal and external business cycle can be automated. But automation extends beyond tactical goals. What are the best profitability strategies? What new markets make the most sense? How should we innovate? When we increase the range of algorithmic applications across supervised to unsupervised machine learning, we can move from tactical to strategic automation.

Just like almost everything, all of this will end up in the cloud. In time, intelligent companies will automate fully in the cloud. Note that the major cloud providers – *AWS*, *Azure*, *Google* and *IBM* – already offer robotic process automation (RPA) services of one kind or another. There will be more.

Post-Covid-19 – and forever – companies will shift their platform thinking *from* large centralised, standardised and integrated enterprise applications *to* platforms that automate business processes and models independent of a single application. While ERP vendors rush to automate their functions, other vendors will take a very different approach. They will identify and model business problems; map and optimise business processes (via process mining) well beyond the processes embedded in ERP applications; identify, collect, validate and leverage structured and unstructured data; match problems, processes, data and machine learning algorithms; and extend the approach to as many known, new and anticipated processes as possible. They will pursue all this outside the boundaries and constraints of their ERP applications. As long as ERP-based "automation" is confined to the automation of processes embedded in the ERP application itself, the ERP world will lag behind next generation digital transformation as it transforms to digital automation.

The example illustrates the movement toward ERP automation, *and* the reinvention of ERP. Yes, new processes! (Even if ERP vendors are wary of the nature and direction of the changes.)

FIVE STEPS TO DIGITAL TRANSFORMATION

Once general requirements are met, there are five steps you can take to increase the chances of transformation success.

First, *map your business with tools – like business process modelling (BPM) – that enable creative, empirical simulations. If you cannot model your existing business processes and your overall business model, you cannot transform anything. Conversely, if your process database is rich, you can transform just about anything.*

Repeatedly run the hypothetical models by changing the variables that point to transformational improvements.

Second, *identify the leverage points in your business models and processes.* Do this by mining empirical data about the costs and benefits of the existing processes and models and through *"what-if"* simulations of alternative improvements. You should also look at what your competitors are doing as well as companies in adjacent industries. If simulation results fall short of measurable transformation, stop testing. Not every company, process or business model will benefit from digital transformation.

Third, *prioritise transformational options.* What's the transformation goal? Is it to save money, increase market share, increase profitability, retain employees, disrupt a company or industry . . . *what?* You must know where you're going to get there. You also need to reality check your prioritised objectives according to budget, time, talent and market constraints: use internal consultants to screen transformation alternatives. From the options list, identify and integrate specific transformation projects to be led by outside brawn.

Fourth, *identify the range of available operational, strategic and emerging technologies that might enable the prioritised transformational options.* Simulate the current and expected technology capabilities to the prioritised transformational functions. Bet on a suite of transformational operational, strategic and emerging technologies.

Fifth, *find leaders with courage.* They're hard to find for all sorts of reasons. If steps one–four have been taken, we can assume that there's a healthy appetite for change, but that change must be tested with widespread support for digital transformation *and* with multi-year financial support. Without supportive leadership and big budgets, nothing will change. Leadership should be demanding: if the ROI on transformational projects is negligible, the projects should be killed. If results achieve or exceed expected ROI, they should be accelerated.

I hope you see the obvious relationship between your business strategy, your business model and the business processes that become the object of your transformation projects. It all turns on the existence and quality of your process data.

DON'T FORGET THE SOFT SIDE

The presence of unambiguous, enthusiastic and continuous support from leadership will make or break every transformation project. One could easily argue that without courageous leadership it makes no sense to take any steps at all. (I could.) At the same time, the business case for digital transformation is generally what leaders need to see before they agree to support a serious transformation initiative. So, the search for enthusiastic leadership must begin before, during and after transformational program planning.

Note again that, in spite of all the talk, the number of corporate executives, especially in public companies, who really want to transform their companies is small. Remember that the whole idea of "disruption" is an abstraction: how many companies have we seen that have – without duress – successfully transformed their business models? Change is expensive, time-consuming, inexact and painful. It's also a political target: in spite of what best-selling business books and pundits tell us, most human beings despise change, which means that transformation is, by definition, constrained.

It's impossible to overstate the importance of corporate culture in digital transformation. The phrase "culture readiness" is packed with implications. If there's conflict between the goals or processes of digital transformation and the corporate culture, there will be problems, as described by *Deloitte* (2022):

> *"Failure to align the effort with employee values and behaviors can create additional risks to an organization's culture if not managed properly."*

If the transformation initiative is focused, for example, on robotic process automation where jobs will be eliminated (for the sake of profitability), there will be repercussions. Companies should assess their cultural readiness through brutal cultural assessments. One of the best ways to accomplish this is to assess a series of digital transformation outcomes against the culture as measured by focus groups, town halls, private interviews, internal social media discussion boards and surveys.

Another way is to contrast incentives with outcomes anticipating the question, *"So what do I get out of this 'transformation'?"* Candour is essential during the culture readiness assessment. Will there be blood? Always. The company should understand – however reluctantly – that some positions will likely be eliminated, some will be redefined, and some will be downgraded. But it should also understand – and widely communicate – that there will be rewards. If the objectives of digital transformation are modest, then cultural readiness should be adequate. But if transformation is designed to be disruptive (perhaps in response to market shocks), expect major issues to rise that challenge the purpose and outcomes of the transformation work.

The *hard* truth about digital transformation is the easiest to accept. Hardware, software, technologies, business process models and cost–benefit models are all easy to understand. The *soft* truth that's much harder to accept refers to leadership, enthusiasm, corporate culture, employee attitudes, discontentment, incentives and punishment, among lots of other "soft" variables that determine the success or failure of digital transformation projects. Far too many executives, project managers and consultants overweight their attention and funding to the hard variables, which are largely controllable.

So, why are leadership and cultural readiness so under-weighted? Why don't executives ask the tough questions about themselves and their cultural readiness? Part of the reason is simple: it's hard to look straight into a mirror. It's therefore hard to assess a culture as "ready" or not, especially when the culture partly belongs to you. There's also a ton of wishful thinking about both leadership and culture accompanied by the belief that sponsoring executives are absolutely, positively supportive (when they're not) and that sponsors can influence (or manipulate) their cultures (when they can't). Unfortunately, there's little evidence to justify these beliefs. When expectations are set, when teams are assembled and when projects are launched, it's essential to be soft, to weight the importance of leadership and cultural readiness as high as any other variables that might appear in the business case.

DIGITAL TRANSFORMATION PLAYS

Most "digital transformation" is not "transformative". It does not disrupt business ... processes or whole business models. Instead, it's "incremental" or just as often part of a planned technology "modernisation" initiative.

The promise of disruptive digital transformation lies far from incremental or modernisation projects.

Transformation requirements:

- *Data must be plentiful and high-quality. Transformation projects that involve big data analytics and artificial intelligence are especially dependent upon quality data.*

- *The brains around digital transformation – what to transform – are in-house brains. The brawn necessary to execute the projects can be found anywhere.*

- *Disruptive transformation is likely to be enabled by – and in many cases dependent upon – emerging digital technology.*

Transformation steps:

- *First, map your business with tools – like business process modelling (BPM) – that enable creative, empirical simulations.*

- *Second, identify the leverage points in your business models and processes.*

- *Third, prioritise transformational options.*

- *Fourth, identify the range of available operational, strategic and emerging technologies that might enable the prioritised transformational options.*

- *Fifth, find leaders with courage.*

- *Don't forget the soft side.*

CHAPTER 4

PAY EXTRA SPECIAL ATTENTION TO AI AND MACHINE LEARNING

CHAPTER SUMMARY

- *Artificial intelligence (AI) and machine learning (ML) will change your business. Its reach is wide and deep.*
- *AI/ML is a must-know technology – a game changer.*
- *Automation can be achieved in ten steps.*

THE PLAYING FIELD

Artificial intelligence and machine learning. Just the words evoke all kinds of reactions, which can range from fear to intense desire. As I described in Chapter 2:

> *"The applications of AI/ML to business models and processes are endless. AI/ML focus on the automation of business processes and tasks, intelligent decision making, predictive analytics, personalisation, and conversational interfaces, among many other areas. The elements of AI include machine learning, natural language processing, algorithms, computer vision, image recognition and robotics . . . AI/ML can literally change your business processes and possibly your entire business model."*

van Duin and Bakhshi (2017) present the range of AI and machine learning in Figure 13.

Here's more about AI and machine learning:

- *Machine learning* is just that. Humans teach a machine how to perform tasks often by just showing the machine how the tasks are performed. For example, the task of granting or rejecting a loan is a very straightforward process full of steps humans take all the time. The steps can be modelled and defined, such as looking at an individual's credit score. Machines can be taught to take this step and find the data necessary to enable the credit-checking task. In this example, machines (with algorithms) can be taught how to mimic human behaviour such that humans no longer have to be involved in the loan approval process.

- *Deep learning* "learns" by finding structures within large sets of data using tools like neural networks (modelled on the human brain) that process data with computational layers designed to identify, classify and predict outcomes. Neural networks simulate human brains and how brains process information in multiple steps. There

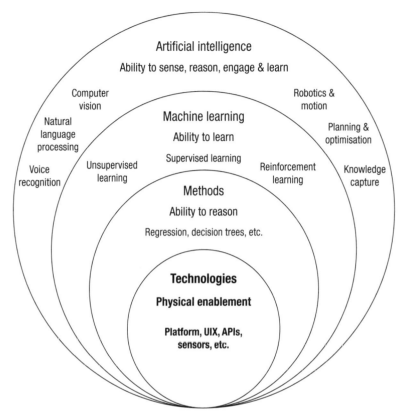

Figure 13 AI and machine learning
From van Duin and Bakhshi.

are several major kinds of neural networks, such as convolutional neural networks.

■ *Algorithms (see Figure 14)* are formulae that solve specific classification and inference problems. There are all sorts of algorithms that range from multiple regression to neutral networks. Algorithms should be viewed as rules, procedures or instructions to be followed to solve problems. Data stimulates algorithms which, once activated, solve problems.

■ *Natural language processing* includes natural language understanding and natural language generation where "machines" understand what they read, what they hear and what they say. Examples include Alexa and Siri – and other personal assistants – which are examples of simple conversational interfaces. Processing massive amounts of text is another application of natural language processing.

■ *Computer vision* enables sensors to "see" images that are then "recognised". In a self-driving car, for example, sensors "see" people, telephone poles, stop lights and baby carriages by "recognising" their features in real-time by matching the features to what it knows about people, telephone poles, stop lights and baby carriages. *Computer vision* and *image recognition* are different steps in the problem-solving process.

Key to understanding AI and machine learning is an understanding of the difference between supervised and unsupervised learning. Supervised learning is the technology we use to "solve" problems that can be modelled and whose "processes" can be trained. For example, if you want to decide who gets a loan and who doesn't, there are criteria you can use to determine if the applicant is loan-worthy (or not), such as their credit history, their income and their net worth. These criteria can be used to train an intelligent system about loan-worthiness. The system will repeat the process endlessly, regardless of whether humans are involved or not. Other problems with the same characteristics – such as admitting students to colleges – can be solved the same way.

More formally, supervised learning can be described as follows (IBM, 2020):

"Supervised learning uses a training set to teach models to yield the desired output. This training dataset includes inputs and correct outputs, which allow the model to learn over time . . . supervised learning can be separated into two types of problems when data mining – classification and regression:

■ *"Classification uses an algorithm to accurately assign test data into specific categories. It recognizes specific entities within the dataset and attempts to draw some conclusions on how those entities should be labelled or defined.*

■ *"Regression is used to understand the relationship between dependent and independent variables. It is commonly used to make projections, such as for sales revenue for a given business."*

Unsupervised learning is quite different (IBM, 2020):

"Unsupervised learning . . . uses machine learning algorithms to analyze and cluster unlabeled datasets. These algorithms discover hidden patterns or data groupings without the need for human intervention. Its ability to discover similarities and differences in information make it the ideal solution for exploratory data analysis, cross-selling strategies, customer segmentation, and image recognition."

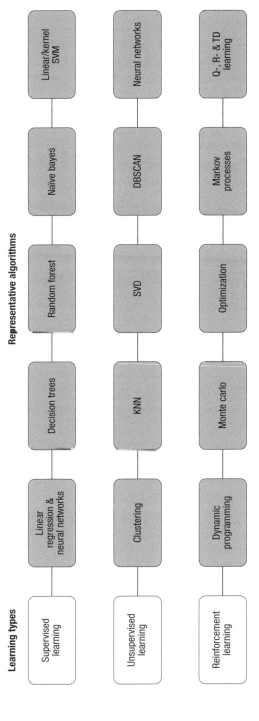

Figure 14 AI and machine learning algorithms

Did you know, for example, that people who are habitually late for meetings are more likely to default on loans than people who are punctual? This correlation was discovered by dumping data into a lake and looking for patterns – which is an example of unsupervised learning.

Algorithms power intelligent systems, as suggested by Figure 14.

Intelligent systems use a variety of algorithms to solve all sorts of problems. Think about algorithms as formulae. They power applications defined around processes, like loan approvals, admissions to colleges, promotions – whatever you want to improve or automate. There are hundreds of them. You don't need to understand them all – they're brawn. The brains here require an understanding what AI and machine learning can and cannot do, and the applications to which they're best suited. Translation? Which as-is/to-be processes will be improved, automated, eliminated and invented by AI and machine learning?

APPLICATION TARGETS (AKA "USE CASES")

The range of applications is staggering. *All* the vertical industries and the models and businesses that enable them are targets. AI will profoundly impact healthcare, transportation, accounting, finance, manufacturing, customer service, aviation, education, sales, marketing, law, entertainment, media, security, negotiation, agriculture, war and peace. No industry or process is safe from the impact that AI and machine learning – across all of its components – will have in the short-run and especially over the next seven to ten years. Keep in mind also that AI and machine learning will integrate across business and technology architectures, databases and applications.

The timing – as always with the enterprise adoption of emerging technologies – is debatable – and the changes will not all be good. Note the ease with which fake news can be created and disseminated by intelligent "news" creators, and how easy it is for smart bots to amplify personal and professional confirmation biases intended to manipulate thinking and behaviour. At the same time, good bots will make much of our personal and professional lives more efficient and productive, freeing us to pursue other activities. Will AI eliminate jobs (see below)? Of course, and this time the elimination of jobs will include so-called knowledge workers as well as the traditional manufacturing jobs we associate with automation and robotics. Much of this capability will arrive simultaneously across whole industries, such as the automotive industry, which will utilise robotics to manufacture driverless cars and then manage their movement across cities and towns across the world.

Similarly, healthcare will be impacted by lifestyles, monitoring, diagnosis and treatment. For example, health diagnostics is already under way for glucose monitoring and heart performance. Based on observed data, treatment can be prescribed. Physicians will read the same data as patients – and prescribe treatments based on the data. Can this be automated? Absolutely.

AI will augment and replace many of us in the workplace. Again, it's a question of *when,* not *if,* but the impact will be sweeping and will likely happen much faster than many analysts predict. Regardless of how bullish or bearish you are about displacement, it's safe to say that millions of jobs – *and knowledge-based careers* – will be impacted and, in many cases, eliminated in the next five-to-seven years.

Investments in all things intelligent are unprecedented. All of the major technology companies are heavily investing in the technology, but the most important investment portfolio belongs to whole countries that have declared AI as a strategic national objective. China, for example, has defined AI as one of its core industries (Knight, 2018).

If your company is not already investing in AI, it's way past time. Not surprisingly, step one is the modelling of your current and aspirational processes informed generously by the potential of AI and machine learning and predictions about the evolution of your industry. *As always, process models should be developed, tested, simulated and inventoried to inform your AI pilot agenda.*

The simplest way to build the automation agenda is to identify the processes most amenable to AI and simulate – through prototyping – the impact intelligent systems might have on the costs and benefits of the target processes. The most robust simulations should rank-order the processes that should be piloted with new technologies.

CEOs, COOs, CIOs and CTOs – among countless chiefs – cannot wait to deploy applications that will save them time and money – *especially money they now spend on humans.* They see AI as a cost manager *and* a profit centre – though some still need convincing – which is your job.

But before we identify all of the application targets, let's first ask the question you really want me to answer:

*"Will AI and machine learning take **my** job and kill **my** career?"*

Well, it depends on what you do for a living, how old you are, where you live and your educational credentials. If you perform routine tasks or even what appear to be complex deductive inferential tasks we associate with "knowledge" industries, yes, your job and career are at significant risk: AI and robotic process automation (RPA) will absolutely, positively threaten your job, your career and your very professional existence. It would be naïve and irresponsible for me to say otherwise – just as it was naïve and irresponsible to tell horse breeders and coach manufacturers that automobiles were no threat at all, or minicomputer manufacturers that desktop computers would not threaten their markets – because, you know, *"there is no reason for any individual to have a computer in his home"* (Wikipedia, 2022; I'm still stunned by this statement made by the CEO – Ken Olsen – of one of the premier minicomputer companies of the twentieth century – the *Digital Equipment Corporation* [though he told everyone that the statement was made out of context]).

Let's also not believe for a moment that automation and low-level AI – combined with lower global labour costs – have been quiet over the past couple of decades. Automation (broadly defined) has already eliminated millions of jobs and redefined whole industries. While new jobs and industries have definitely been created during this time, the transitional pain was huge and will likely increase throughout the rest of the twenty-first century – *and forever,* as technology continues its relentless march to some version of productivity singularity.

McKinsey & Co. predicts that AI (broadly defined) will eliminate 75,000,000 jobs over the next 20 years (Vlastelica, 2017):

> *"Our scenarios suggest that by 2030, 75 million to 375 million workers (3 to 14 percent of the global workforce) will need to switch occupational categories."*

Bloomberg has developed a tool to help you determine if you're likely to be automated (Whitehouse and Rojanasakul, 2017). According to *Bloomberg's* research (based in part on research conducted at the *University of Oxford*):

> *"Nearly half of all U.S. jobs may be at risk in the coming decades, with lower-paid occupations among the most vulnerable."*

Compensation and benefits managers, auditors, accountants, credit analysts, loan officers, sales representatives, truck drivers, administrative services managers and even some dental hygienists are at high risk and *"most likely to be automated".* Some analysts believe significant professional displacement will occur by 2030, while others believe it will take longer. (It won't take longer.)

Now let's flip the question.

If you can, forget about the impact on your career and look at the most vulnerable occupations as opportunities for you to save money and make money with AI and machine learning. Harsh, I know. But everyone wants to lower costs, and enormous costs are wrapped around people.

Way back in 2013, Carl Benedikt Frey and Michael A. Osborne published a report titled "The Future of Employment: How Susceptible are Jobs to Computerisation?" (Frey and Osborne, 2013).

Here's their list of the professionals with the *highest replacement risk*:

1. *Data Entry Keyers (99%)*
2. *Cargo and Freight Agents (99%)*
3. *Watch Repairers (99%)*
4. *Title Examiners, Abstractors, and Searchers (99%)*
5. *Telemarketers (99%)*
6. *Tax Preparers (99%)*
7. *Sewers, Hand (99%)*
8. *Photographic Process Workers and Processing Machine Operators (99%)*
9. *New Accounts Clerks (99%)*
10. *Mathematical Technicians (99%)*

Here are the highest paid professionals with the *highest automation risk*:

1. *Compensation and Benefits Managers (96%)*
2. *Nuclear Power Reactor Operators (95%)*
3. *Nuclear Technicians (85%)*
4. *Administrative Services Managers (73%)*
5. *Atmospheric and Space Scientists (67%)*
6. *Power Distributors and Dispatchers (64%)*
7. *Administrative Law Judges, Adjudicators, and Hearing Officers (64%)*
8. *Geoscientists, Except Hydrologists and Geographers (63%)*
9. *Transportation, Storage, and Distribution Managers (59%)*
10. *Personal Financial Advisors (58%)*

And the professions with the *lowest risk*?

1. *Recreational Therapists (0.28%)*
2. *First-Line Supervisors of Mechanics, Installers and Repairers (0.30%)*

3. *Emergency Management Directors (0.30%)*
4. *Mental Health and Substance Abuse Social Workers (0.31%)*
5. *Audiologists (0.33%)*
6. *Orthotists and Prosthetists (0.35%)*
7. *Occupational Therapists (0.35%)*
8. *Healthcare Social Workers (0.35%)*
9. *Oral and Maxillofacial Surgeons (0.36%)*
10. *First-Line Supervisors of Fire Fighting and Prevention Workers (0.36%)*

Much more recent analyses (Saviom, 2021) essentially agree with the above lists, *which means we knew this was coming well over a decade ago.*

The most brutal question is how many of these professionals are in your workforce? Tasks that are repetitive, well defined – "well bounded" in automation terminology – deductive inferential-based tasks surrounded by accessible quantitative-empirical data are at the highest risk (or opportunity) for automation. Business process modelling and mining (BPM^2) can be used to determine the extent the processes can be automated. If the processes reveal a large number of repetitive, well-bounded, deductive tasks, for example, then robotic process automation (RPA) will be applied.

Will software "robots" save you money and increase your efficiency? If the job has the characteristics described above, yes. The only question left is how long it will take you to collect the savings and efficiency.

Precise timelines about the arrival of automated solutions across industries are impossible to make. But what we *can* make are predictions about how welcome automation will be across a number of industries, including the ones where the greatest resignations are occurring – and especially in many human-intensive ones, such as fast food and agriculture.

For example, fast food restaurants are investing heavily in automation (Sozzi, 2021):

> *"Fast-food's biggest players are letting the robots right in through the front door as they seek out ways to overcome rising wages and worker shortages."*

As reported by Sozzi:

> *"McDonald's . . . is testing automated voice ordering for . . . (and) looking at better ways to automate the kitchen . . .*
>
> *"Domino's . . . struck a deal with self-driving delivery company Nuro . . .*
>
> *"Taco Bell . . . in New York City . . . (is) built . . . to get your food (with) . . . minimal interaction with an employee . . . "*

Agriculture is one of the most aggressive targets of automation. Robotics are already having impact on the industry. Some examples (thanks to Donovan Alexander's reporting in *Interesting Engineering*, 2021):

> *"Ecorobotix: the robot uses its complex camera system to target and spray weeds . . .*
>
> *"Energid Citrus Picking System: can pick a fruit every 2 to 3 seconds . . .*
>
> *"Agrobot E-Series: with . . . twenty-four robotic arms . . . can not only pick strawberries really fast, but it can identify the ripeness of a strawberry in the field."*

Are you in these industries? If you are, opportunity is everywhere.

The examples above are in just two industries, but automation doesn't stop there.

- Do we need tax preparers? (No.)
- Car salesmen? (God, no.)
- Loan officers? (Never did.)

The incentives are clear. Why wouldn't *Uber* want to eliminate its biggest headache – drivers – with autonomous vehicles? Why wouldn't companies want to deploy "workers" that work 24/7, never need vacations and never get sick?

> *"Efficiencies? Honeywell (2021) reports some survey results: "The productivity gains that we see from . . . robotics has increased . . . that's because a warehouse that might typically require 2,000 workers could deploy technologies and warehouse execution software to instead operate with only 200 . . . robotic technologies directly replace labor, whether it be unloading trucks, picking orders, fulfilling orders . . . "*

We must also admit that machines can do many things better than humans (Ghosh, 2018). Medical scans, loan processing and health diagnoses are just three areas where machines perform better than humans. In time, the number of tasks where machines will outperform humans will only grow. Like this (University of Oxford, 2019):

> *"Technology developed using artificial intelligence (AI) could identify people at high risk of a fatal heart attack at least five years before it strikes, according to new research funded by the British Heart Foundation (BHF). The findings are being presented at the European Society of Cardiology (ESC) Congress in Paris and published in the European Heart Journal."*

There's so much more here – like medical imaging, diagnosis, drug discovery, radiation treatment and genomics, among many other areas. Humans should select and deploy the ones with the greatest impact and lowest cost – now.

The legal profession (LawGeex, 2017)?

> *"Twenty US-trained lawyers, with decades of legal experience ranging from law firms to corporations, were asked to issue-spot legal issues in five standard NDAs. They competed against a LawGeex AI system that has been developed for three years and trained on tens of thousands of contracts. The research was conducted with input from academics, data scientists, and legal and machine-learning experts, and was overseen by an independent consultant and lawyer . . . following extensive testing, the LawGeex Artificial Intelligence achieved an average 94% accuracy rate, ahead of the lawyers who achieved an average rate of 85%."*

Finance (Sergeenkov, 2019)?

> *"A research team from the University of Erlangen-Nuremberg has developed a number of algorithms that use historical data from markets to replicate real-time investments. One of the models allowed for a 73% return on investment annually from 1992 to 2015. This compares with a real market return of 9% per year. Profits were particularly high during the market shocks of 2000 (a 545% yield) and 2008 (a 681% yield)."*

War (Lee, 2021)?

We already know that drones are often the weapons of choice in many situations. We also know that robots are being groomed to replace human soldiers. Tacticians and strategists will be automated. Intelligent weapons systems will become the most loyal, effective soldiers countries employ.

Transportation?

The *Los Angeles Times* predicts (Baral, 2021) that *"Self-driving trucks could replace 1.7 million American truckers in the next ten years."*

Opportunity is everywhere. *Which of your as-is and to-be processes are ready for automation?*

TEN STEPS TO AUTOMATION

The spectre of automation still frightens many executives, especially executives of a certain age and demographic. It's a disruptive possibility and, in spite of what technology evangelists believe, can be threatening to technology managers and executives. All decision-makers – including

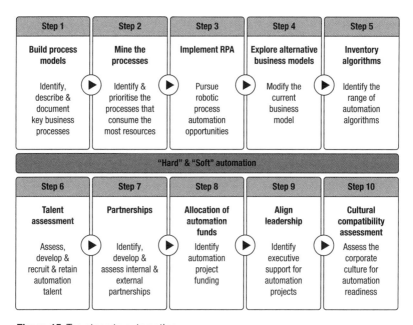

Figure 15 Ten steps to automation
From Andriole and *IEEE IT Professional*.
Andriole, SJ (2022) "Automation is a 10-Step Competitive Necessity." Published in: IEEE IT Professional (Volume: 24, Issue: 1, 01 Jan. Feb. 2022) DOI: 10.1109/MITP.2021.3136017

you – would like to reduce costs and increase revenue. There's a way to do just that, as illustrated in Figure 15. But business cases around automation should speak directly to cost reduction and revenue generation. If the business case is weak, the steps proposed here will never be taken.

Note the continued relevance of business process modelling, mining and management. Remember that processes descend from the business model which descends from the overall business strategy. It's all connected, and it's all pretty simple.

STEP 1: PROCESS MODELLING

The first step is the development of an inventory of internal and external business processes that describe how their companies operate. As discussed in Chapter 1, most companies do not have process inventories, so companies must identify and describe their operational and strategic processes for manual inspection or, ideally, through software-based process mining. This step provides the hook, evidence that the company is spending a ton of money on processes that may not be necessary, or that the processes themselves can be automated, resulting in headcount reduction *and* greater efficiency.

STEP 2: PROCESS MINING

The next step is the identification of the most expensive processes and the processes that take the longest to execute. As discussed in Chapter 1, there are tools that perform this task automatically (from vendors such as *UiPath* and *Celonis*). Process mining tools provide *"visibility into current processes and the vulnerabilities or gaps within those processes. From there, it enables users to create data-driven improvements based on how these processes are actually conducted."* This step is critical to the automation process.

STEP 3: ROBOTIC PROCESS AUTOMATION

Robotic process automation (RPA) enables the automation of the processes with the highest cost/impact leverage. Many of the same vendors offer RPA tools. Everyone likes RPA because it operationalises purposeful process management where they can see where processes can be modified, eliminated or automated. It's where cost savings become real, and it's also where whole new processes are born. This step launches the automation journey.

STEP 4: BUSINESS MODEL EXPLORATION

All this process analysis leads to larger questions about the overall business model of the company. *If lots of business processes should be modified, eliminated and automated, and if lots of new ones should replace the old ones, then maybe the whole business model needs replacing.* Process modelling, process mining and RPA can be steps to automation disruption – and whole new business models. Should *H&R Block* and *Turbotax* automate themselves out of their current business before a new entrant does? Should universities leave the classroom and retire their sages-on-the-stage? These are the kinds of questions you should ask as you inspect your business model.

STEP 5: ALGORITHMIC INTELLIGENCE

Algorithmic intelligence is also necessary. Artificial intelligence and machine learning achieve automation by training data and applying algorithms to narrow, generalised and deep learning-defined problems. Some of the algorithms (in Figure 14) include classification, regression and clustering algorithms, and some of the specific algorithms in these classes include (for classification), naïve Bayes, Random Forest, Nearest Neighbour and Decision Trees, among others. For regression, the list includes Linear Logistic, Lasso and Multivariate Regression, among others; and for clustering, the list might include Fuzzy C-Means, K-Means and Hierarchical Clustering algorithms, among others. These lists illustrate the range and complexity of the algorithmic options available to automate business processes and entire business models. Algorithmic intelligence is also a brains versus brawn issue, where executives, managers and decision-makers should understand the range and power of algorithms, but not exactly how they work or how they can be implemented in intelligent applications, which is a brawn capability.

STEP 6: TALENT ASSESSMENT

We'll look more closely at the talent problem in Chapter 9, but you should take a hard look at your AI and machine learning talent. You should rate your company's ability to automate processes and business models. Given how new some of the technologies are, and how frequently new ones appear, you will likely discover that your automation bench is weak. If this is the case, a concerted effort to recruit talent into the organisation should begin. *If recruitment stalls, there's no chance automation will succeed.*

STEP 7: PARTNERSHIP DEVELOPMENT

No matter how successful a company's recruitment efforts are, brawn partners will be necessary to automate processes and especially entire business models. Internal and external partners are required. Internally, the strategy, technology, products and services professionals should be involved in all automation plans. Externally, a stable of vendors experienced with automation should be developed, noting that all external relationships should be temporary, routinely replaced with new vendors with deeper and more relevant experience. No long-term commitments to any automation vendors. A classic brains versus brawn calculation.

STEP 8: FUNDING

Like so many of the business-technology projects in this book, all this must be funded. Automation is not a "science project" that might, over time, yield some interesting results. Automation is a variable cost that should be adjusted at least annually. If there's no money to automate, then all's for naught. What about a Centre of Excellence for AI and machine learning? Yes. Strongly consider one, especially if you're in an industry with models and processes just waiting to be automated.

STEP 9: EXECUTIVE LEADERSHIP

Without executive support for automation, no one will take the initiative seriously. Support comes in many forms including funding, internal and external communications, recruitment and repeatable processes for innovating around automation. It also requires ongoing support even when projects fail to return immediate value. If you're that executive, fund and support the hell out of your AI and machine learning initiatives.

STEP 10: CULTURAL COMPATIBILITY

This is perhaps the most challenging step. It requires you to objectively assess the corporate culture to determine its compatibility with innovation, especially innovation focused on automation. There's often a larger issue at work here. While you may talk a good digital game, you may not walk the walk. Step 10 requires you to control old technology antibodies and allow automation to spread throughout the business model and its enabling processes.

AN OVERDUE CAPABILITY ("IF I COULD TALK TO THE ANIMALS")

Remember when Rex Harrison sang about talking to the animals as Dr Dolittle (YouTube, 2006)? Of course you don't but trust me when I remind you that it's still a memorable song in some circles. Let me adjust the emphasis. If I could talk to smart (and not so smart) applications, so much would be better. Take bots. Everyone knows that bots are stupid. They're also annoying. I have no idea why a company would develop and launch a customer service bot they know will frustrate their customers. Actually, I do – and so do you. It enables them to reduce the number of human agents they pay with actual money – even though they know their customers prefer talking to humans.

So how do people feel about bots? If bots immediately solve a customer's problem, they're more than acceptable alternatives to waiting on the phone to speak to a human customer service representative (CSR) – especially if the CSR is incompetent. On the other hand, if the bot cannot quickly solve a customer's problem, then dissatisfaction skyrockets. This line is about as binary as it gets: fix the problem quickly or go away. Since many bots have limited capabilities, customers find themselves asking for a CSR which can take a long time within a chat session. Leaving the session to start a phone-based process is equally frustrating because of wait times. At the end of the day, frustration is almost inevitable. Chatbots save companies a ton of money and customer dissatisfaction is a small price to pay for the enormous savings bots can generate, especially since customers are unlikely to leave a vendor because of a bad bot experience.

Like you, I've had horrible experiences. Chatbots are often incredibly dumb and circular. The flawed design is astounding. Many bots present a menu from which you choose a problem area, but once you select one – and respond "other" – you're looped back to the same menu. Over and over again.

Are bots improving? They are, especially in well-bounded areas where questions can be semi-accurately predicted. But, as soon as a customer leaves the script, well, that's when frustration skyrockets. The requisite skill? Knowing how to get human agents by tricking bots into a handoff. But that's not the answer.

PIECES OF CONVERSATION

When you converse with a human, here are the abilities you assume (Changing Minds, 2017):

> *"Asking: Engaging and seeking information.*
>
> *Informing: Giving information.*
>
> *Asserting: Stating something as true.*
>
> *Proposing: Putting forward argument.*
>
> *Summarizing: Reflecting your understanding.*
>
> *Checking: Testing understanding.*
>
> *Building: Adding to existing ideas.*
>
> *Including: Bringing in others.*
>
> *Excluding: Shutting out others.*

Self-promotion: Boosting oneself.

Supporting: Lending strength.

Disagreeing: Refusing to agree.

Avoiding: Refusing to consider argument.

Challenging: Offering new thoughts to change thinking.

Attacking: Destruction of their ideas.

Defending: Stopping their attacks.

Blocking: Putting things in the way of their arguments."

How many "interfaces" have anywhere near these capabilities? Sure, this is too much to expect from a conversational interface but is the general direction correct or incorrect?

CONVERSATIONAL CHATBOT DESIGN

Here's what Cobus Greyling (2020) describes as conversational AI design principles:

- *Take turns speaking . . .*
- *Develop a working persona . . .*
- *Communicate within context . . .*
- *Manage conversational intent . . .*
- *Adapt to conversational variation . . .*
- *Inform . . .*
- *Keep dialog on track . . .*
- *Move conversations forward . . .*
- *Stick to domains . . .*

These design principles are solid. They move us toward human-to-human communication but in a machine, which is the goal. Singularity issues aside, this is what we want and need – however "simulated" (for now) it might be. We must respect technological limitations while always pushing in the right direction.

CONVERSATIONAL AI TO THE RESCUE

When I need help, the app should "understand" me, what I mean, what I need and what a perfect outcome should be (in multiple languages in real time). Is that too much to ask? Today it is. But that's where this needs to go – and not just for customer service, but for all interaction with intelligent systems. The experience should also be proactive where applications tell me what I need and how that need has already been satisfied. Until we get there, AI and machine learning will be limited to well-bounded, deductive inferential tasks – what we call supervised learning with tons of labelled data that invokes linear regression to repeat human decision making. While this is OK, it's not what humans ultimately want or need. Supervised learners are today's slaves. We want partners!

INCREDIBLE STRENGTHS AND SOME LIMITATIONS

As I've already argued, AI and machine learning is transforming personal and professional processes at a pace I never anticipated. I believe it's the most important technology (thus far) of the twenty-first century. The dirty little secret? Yes, most of the most-powerful applications are in well-bounded domains where supervised learning with regression is the preferred approach. The field needs more before it truly transforms our personal and professional lives. Conversational AI is a huge step in that direction. We need to get there before the bots kill us with anger and frustration.

POSTSCRIPT: THE SINGULARITY

What about all the fuss about "the singularity"?

Predictions about the arrival of the singularity — when machines become smarter than humans — vary, of course, but I have another perspective which essentially welcomes super-intelligence into our worlds. Is it horrific and threatening when the best doctors are machines, or when machines provide universal healthcare (in the USA), or when drug discoveries and genomic research are enabled by machines? Of course, these "machines" can be abused, but if the singularists are right, then the machines will self-correct – as superior intellects will do – and avoid some of the major disasters that have plagued humans for centuries. Without getting overly philosophical, why shouldn't humans welcome and partner with expanded intelligence regardless of its form? Especially when, according to subscribers of the singularity, we have no choice. So until the machine intelligence explosion occurs, perhaps we should worry more about the explosions that have killed millions of humans over the years and look to smart machines to help us live longer and better lives. If they can free us from tedium, help us stay healthier and propel us toward a safer future, I don't think we should fear them at least until they become as lethal as the "intelligence" we face today.

POST-POSTSCRIPT: GENERATIVE AI

One of the most important developments in AI and machine learning is generative AI which refers to machine intelligence that can generate new and novel content on its own. Some of this content includes art, music, marketing plans, strategies, images, code and even relationship advice. Note that Generative AI uses unsupervised learning algorithms to "create." The output feels authentic and accurate — almost scary — but there are limitations not always obvious to new users of tools like ChatGPT. The advice here is to track progress in this area extremely closely. Generative capabilities will only increase over time and may solve many problems that have been beyond the capabilities of "conventional" AI.

AI AND MACHINE LEARNING PLAYS

AI and machine learning can literally change your business processes and, possibly, your entire business model. Why? Intelligent systems save money and make money. The range of applications is staggering, including all of the vertical industries and every business process and model that supports them. AI will profoundly impact healthcare, transportation, accounting, finance, manufacturing, customer service, aviation, education, sales, marketing, law, entertainment, media, security, negotiation, war and peace.

BPM[3] can be used to determine the extent target processes can be automated. If the processes reveal a large number of repetitive, well-bounded, deductive tasks, for example, then RPA can be applied. Ten steps can help:

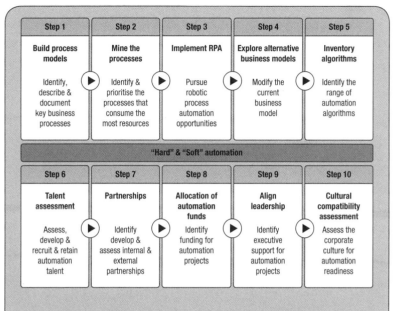

Step 1	Step 2	Step 3	Step 4	Step 5
Build process models	**Mine the processes**	**Implement RPA**	**Explore alternative business models**	**Inventory algorithms**
Identify, describe & document key business processes	Identify & prioritise the processes that consume the most resources	Pursue robotic process automation opportunities	Modify the current business model	Identify the range of automation algorithms

"Hard" & "Soft" automation

Step 6	Step 7	Step 8	Step 9	Step 10
Talent assessment	**Partnerships**	**Allocation of automation funds**	**Align leadership**	**Cultural compatibility assessment**
Assess, develop & recruit & retain automation talent	Identify develop & assess internal & external partnerships	Identify funding for automation projects	Identify executive support for automation projects	Assess the corporate culture for automation readiness

Consider a Center of Excellence (COE) if your industry is comprised of processes ripe for automation.

Don't worry about the singularity.

Track progress in generative AI extremely closely.

CHAPTER 5

INVEST WHAT YOU MUST IN CYBERSECURITY

CHAPTER SUMMARY

- *The number and severity of cyberattacks is growing.*
- *"Bots" are the foot soldiers of cyberwarfare.*
- *There are audit-approved best practices to reduce the number of cyberattacks.*
- *There are "diabolical" aspects of cyberwarfare and cybersecurity that explain under-investments in cybersecurity.*
- *Invest in "just enough" cybersecurity.*

CYBERWARFARE

The number and severity of cyberattacks continues to grow. Cyberwarfare has now levelled the playing field in industry, government and national defence: why spend tons of money on an aircraft carrier when you can disable it digitally? Why spend billions on new product R&D when you can hack into your competition's strategic plans? Why not just phish around municipalities for a quick $100k?

Cyberwarfare is a cost-effective solution to all sorts of problems – and opportunities: cyberwarfare is a revenue stream, a new business model, a weapon and digital transformation with its own unique flavour. The whole world is warning anyone who will listen about cyberwarfare. Why? Because it's the cheapest, easiest, fastest and most effective form of warfare we've ever seen, and because cyberwarfare defences are more vulnerable than they've ever been. Is any of this about to change?

Listen to what Daniel Markuson (2020) at *NordVPN* predicts:

> *"Healthcare is at the risk of becoming the most breached sector. These organizations deal with great amounts of sensitive data but often fail to apply the latest security standards. Misconfigured databases and back-ups will be the leading reasons for successful hacker attacks. Hackers will get more creative, using complex social engineering techniques on potential victims. A significant increase in business email compromise and ransomware is predicted too."*

Cybersecurity firm *Trend Micro* (2020) has more predictions:

- *"Attackers will outpace incomplete and hurried patches.*
- *"Cybercriminals will turn to blockchain platforms for their transactions in the underground.*

- *"Banking systems will be in the crosshairs with open banking and ATM malware.*

- *"Deepfakes will be the next frontier for enterprise fraud.*

- *"Managed service providers will be compromised for malware distribution and supply chain attacks.*

- *"Attackers will capitalize on 'wormable' flaws and deserialization bugs.*

- *"Cybercriminals will home in on IoT devices for espionage and extortion.*

- *"5G adopters will grapple with the security implications of moving to software-defined networks.*

- *"Critical infrastructures will be plagued by more attacks and production downtimes.*

- *"Home offices and other remote-working setups will redefine supply chain attacks underscoring the need for security throughout the deployment pipeline.*

- *"Vulnerabilities in container components will be top security concerns for DevOps teams.*

- *"Serverless platforms will introduce an attack surface for misconfiguration and vulnerable codes.*

- *"User misconfigurations and unsecure third-party involvement will compound risks in cloud platforms.*

- *"Cloud platforms will fall prey to code injection attacks via third-party libraries.*

- *"Predictive and behavioral detection will be crucial against persistent and fileless threats.*

- *"The MITRE ATT&CK Framework (2022) will play a bigger role in how enterprises assess security.*

- *"Threat intelligence will need to be augmented with security analytics expertise for protection across security layers."*

There are other lists just as long and just as threatening. So why is cybersecurity still underfunded? Why are the number and severity of cyberattacks growing?

Years ago, my responsibilities as CTO included an assessment of the security architecture and the company's digital vulnerabilities. When my team finished its assessment, the results were scary. When I took the results to the CFO (to which technology reported), his first and only question was, *"What's this going to cost me?"* which of course was exactly the wrong question.

Or was it?

Seems like an open and shut case for funding. *Seems like.* (We'll return to this disconnect later in the chapter. Suffice it to say now that there may be some diabolical factors that explain why there's so much underspending in cybersecurity.)

Until then (!), everyone must develop both offensive and defensive cyber capabilities. Competitiveness depends upon digital security on every level. Without security, governments and companies cannot operate. Public companies are especially vulnerable because they have shareholders and (sometimes) responsible boards of directors looking after shareholders.

Even the popular US weekly television show *60 Minutes* thinks the *SolarWinds* attack was a big deal (2021). *60 Minutes* examined the *Solar-Winds* – remember? – breach. The segment felt like a voice crying in the wilderness. As a business-technology professional, I was stunned to hear descriptions of how the attack occurred. But what stunned me the most was when one of the experts said the only way to guarantee the problem was completely resolved is to replace all the computers it touched (more on this in a moment, so prepare). I was immediately reminded of the CFO's question: *"What's this all going to cost me?"*.

CYBERWARFARE → CYBERATTACKS

Let's level set. There are numerous kinds of cyberattacks and best practices about how to reduce their occurrence and impact. Let's start with motivation (Ecosystm, 2019):

- Financial gain
- Hacktivism – political or social
- Intellectual challenge
- Espionage
- Organised cyber crime
- Disruption.

Now let's look at the specific kinds of cyberattacks that define cyberwarfare (Ecosystm, 2019):

> *"**Malware** is a type of cyberattack where malicious software is installed on the victim's systems through executable files usually*

without the user's knowledge. Malware includes malicious software, including spyware, ransomware, viruses, and worms.

*"**Phishing** refers to spoofing or deceptive communications activities performed by the attackers that appear to originate from a credible source such as emails, messages, legitimate websites that are disguised. Through phishing, attackers try to fetch sensitive information, user details, credit card numbers or make fraudulent attempts.*

*"**Man-in-the-middle** attacks . . . happen with relaying or altering the communication channels. This can be communication between organizations and cloud server or over unsecured networks.*

*"**DoS/DDoS** attack(s) aim at flooding the target website with over-whelming traffic to exhaust resources and bandwidth of the system. These are not to bring down a website but to breach a security perimeter and smoke out the online systems. This can reduce a user base or may bring down the entire network.*

*"**SQL Injection** . . . inject(s) a nefarious code or statements into SQL queries or a database server to extract information from the database or to take a data dump of the complete database.*

*"**Zero-day** is a software security flaw which is known to the software developers. Attackers try to exploit a vulnerability before a patch or solution is implemented to capture the system with known weaknesses.*

*"**Cross Site Scripting** . . . attacks occur when a web app sends malicious code in the form of a side script to another user thus bypassing access controls of the site to same as the origin.*

*"**Business Email Compromise** . . . is an attack to spoof business emails and gain illegal access to company accounts and ids to defraud the company or its employees."*

BOTS AND CYBERWARFARE

The cyberwarfare/cyberattack/cybersecurity world is enabled by bots. In fact, nearly half of all web traffic is from "bots". That statistic alone should grab your attention, but the one that should worry you more is that "bad bots" are growing in number, reach and impact. They're also getting smarter. But what *are* "bots?" A bot (Digital Guide Ionos, 2022):

"Is an automated program that is programmed for certain actions and executes them either regularly or reactively. The bot does this without

needing human activation. It analyzes the environment and 'decides' which actions to take depending on the situation."

Bots are "good" and "bad". Some good bots include (Luksza, 2018):

"Crawlers/Spiders – Used by search engines and online services to discover and index website content, making it easier for internet users to find it.

"Traders (Bitcoin trading bots) – Used by Ecommerce businesses to act like agents on behalf of humans, interacting with external systems to accomplish a specific transaction, moving data from one platform to another. Based on the given pricing criteria, they search for the best deals and then automatically buy or sell.

"Monitoring Bots – Monitor health system of the website, evaluate its accessibility, report on page load times & downtime duration, keeping it healthy and responsive.

"Feedfetcher/Informational – Collect information from different websites to keep the users or subscribers up to date on the news, events or blog articles. They cover different forms of content fetching, from updating weather conditions to censoring language in comments and chat rooms.

"Chat Bots – A service that enables interacting with a user via a chat interface regarding a number of things, ranging from functional to fun."

Some bad bots include (also from Luksza, 2018):

"Impersonators – Designed to mimic human behavior to bypass the security and by following offsite commands, steal or bring down the website. This category also includes propaganda bots, used by countries to manipulate public opinion.

"Scrapers – Scrape and steal original content and relevant information. Often repost it on other websites. Scrapers can reverse-engineer pricing, product catalogues and business models or steal customers lists and email addresses for spam purposes.

"Spammers – Post phishing links and low-quality promotional content to lure visitors away from the website and ultimately drive traffic to the spammer's website. Often use malware or black hat SEO techniques that may lead to blacklisting the infected site. A specific type of spammer is auto-refresh bots, which generate fake traffic.

"Click/Download Bots – intentionally interact or click on PPC and performance-based ads. Associated costs of such ads increase

based on exposure to an ad – meaning the more people are reached, the more expensive they are."

Bots work 24/7 behind the scenes, though they're not completely stealthy. In fact, they're discoverable (DFRLab, 2017). At the same time, they're getting smarter. The marriage among bots, artificial intelligence (AI) and machine learning (ML) is yielding smart children of all shapes and sizes. The good news? Smart bots are mostly good. But the bad news is that bad bots are getting really smart. Social bots, for example, have learned to lie with astonishing efficiency.

What happens when social bots begin to learn and adapt? What happens when they understand every language? What happens when they cannot be fooled? What happens when they become emotionally intelligent (Manning, 2018)? Or when bot development platforms enable the rapid development of bots who can understand, learn – and plot? (*SAP* already promises the development of intelligent bots in three minutes; Galer, 2018.) But it's not the technologies that will, for example, make chatbots smarter or nastier, how semantic parsing, automated planning and natural language understanding/generation will make bots smarter, but about how these and other foundation technologies will enable the worst kind of bots – "Freddie Kruegerbots" – and what these bots will do.

Bad bots are multiplying – and they're winning: the activity rate for bad bots is higher than good ones. What about Freddie Kruegerbots and *Twitter*? Do they know they're in a war? Or are they waging it?

Victories and losses will be determined by the number and capabilities of bots designed to seek and destroy opponents – which, according to Shelly Palmer (2018), is easier than it may sound:

"Today, using open-source software and some inexpensive cloud services, you can create AI-troll/bot combinations and release armies of them at extremely low cost."

In the good bot space, efficiency and competitive response is essential. In the bad bot space, efficiency *and self-defence* is essential. Bots need to know their competitors and adversaries. Continuous tracking and adaptation are necessary. AI and machine learning will enable good and bad bots, but everyone must fight.

The bot battlefield will play out competitively in crawlers, traders, monitors, chatters, scrapers, spammers and impersonators. Good versus evil? To some extent, yes, and the only ones that can win this war are the bots themselves. Alternatively, there are some who believe that regulatory reform is right around the corner but, based on US testimony and ongoing legislative paralysis, it's hard to see when any meaningful bot regulations will appear. But if there's no legislative remedy, then what? It's bots versus bots – and the cyberwarfare they conduct. As *Webroot* (2022) describes, bad bots are used by cybercriminals to steal financial and personal information, attack legitimate web services and extort money from victims. In fact:

> *"Botnets have been one of the most common methods of malware deployment for the past decade, infecting hundreds of millions of computers. As botnets infect new technologies, such as Internet of Things (IoT) devices in homes, public spaces, and secure areas, compromised systems can put even more unsuspecting users at risk."*

BREACHES

For perspective, here are the biggest data breaches of the twenty-first century – so far (Hill and Swinhoe, 2021; Hill, 2022):

1. *Yahoo* – 3 billion accounts.
2. *Alibaba* – 1.1 billion pieces of user data.
3. *LinkedIn* – 700 million users.
4. *Sina Weibo* – 538 million accounts.
5. *Facebook* – 533 million users.
6. *Marriott International (Starwood)* – 500 million customers.
7. *Yahoo* – 500 million accounts.
8. *Adult Friend Finder* – 412.2 million accounts.
9. *MySpace* – 360 million user accounts.
10. *NetEase* – 235 million user accounts.
11. *Court Ventures* (Experian) – 200 million personal records.
12. *LinkedIn* – 165 million users.
13. *Dubsmash* – 162 million user accounts.
14. *Adobe* – 153 million user records.
15. *My Fitness Pal* – 150 million user accounts.

Breaches occur every day. Imagine how many consumers are impacted by these breaches. Do you think the damage experienced by the companies – *perhaps your company* – was commensurate with the damage inflicted on consumers?

We've been in a serious cyberwar for decades. But can you say exactly where it's being waged and who's fighting whom? Can you describe what cyberwarfare weapons are being used to wage cyberwars? Can you identify who the cyberwarfare superpowers are? Do you know who's winning? You need a team that can answer these questions.

BEST PRACTICES

The industry recommends cybersecurity best practices (Ecosystm, 2019):

*"**Secure assets.** It is always considered a security best practice to keep your systems and infrastructure updated with latest security patches and updates which are released from vendors or manufacturers on a regular basis.*

*"**Conduct threat assessment.** Vulnerabilities can arise within your own system or potentially from other sources which are not directly under your control, but they can be identified if you are aware. Perform regular due diligence of your system or network security.*

*"**Stay informed on threats.** News articles, software companies, cyber security organizations often release information on threats and vulnerabilities that can help you stay informed and act against threats.*

*"**Formulate steps to avoid threats.** Training and regular information to organizations and employees can prevent many attacks from happening. If your users or employees are aware and informed they can escape the threats. Keep strong passwords, encrypt sensitive information, safeguard accounts, use firewalls to prevent attacks.*

*"**Plan an incident response.** Create plans and approaches to react against a cyberattack to manage and limit the damage. Always keep your systems backed up online/offline and prepare your IT team to deal with it. You may also take advice or may hire experts to strengthen your infrastructure security."*

Note that many – if not all – of these steps are required by (internal and external) auditors.

Cyberattacks and cyberwarfare will continue to grow seemingly unchecked. Your challenge is clear. Protect your digital assets as best as possible. But how? With how much money? If your goal is to reduce the number of threats and attacks well below what it is today, you will need some people, some money, a business case, a story and an audience that worries about cybersecurity. There are best practices you can follow that offer the traditional cybersecurity steps. But you also need to fully understand the context of cyberwarfare/cybersecurity, which simultaneously documents attacks while assuming there's a cybersecurity threshold which cannot be crossed, that your success will be limited no matter how much you spend and how many security professionals you hire. Really? Really.

So your response to the barrage of cyberattacks is, by definition, mitigated. With that said, let's look at traditional cybersecurity steps. We'll end the chapter with what you might believe are some cynical plays.

Information Management published some lessons learned from data breaches (2016). Can we learn from these lessons? Maybe. Like so many of the lessons published every year, they rehash what we've known for years. Sorry, there are no *new* best practices here. See what you think (my reactions are clear).

"A Record Year for Data Breaches."

Does anyone believe that the number of data breaches and larger digital security concerns is shrinking?

"The Move to the Cloud Puts Organizations at Greater Risk."

Nothing profound here either. But let's remember that the cloud is just another (virtual) location. The assumption that the cloud brings more risk is obvious, simply because the number of cloud-delivered applications is increasing. Put another way, if the number of internal applications increased as rapidly as cloud deployments have increased, there would be greater risk internally. As the number of applications and data bases increases, digital risk rises proportionately – regardless of where the applications and data bases are located. Stop attacking the cloud as "unsafe". *It's all "unsafe".* As more and more business rules, processes, transactions and whole business models become digital, the greater the risk. Coaches know that the more athletes you play, the more injuries there will be; and the longer the game goes on, the more penalties there will be.

"First and Foremost, Create a Formal Policy Around Insider Threats."

Wow: everyone should have security policies that address insider security threats. If your auditor hasn't already told you this, you need a new auditor. If your CIO, CTO and CISO haven't told you this, you need a new CIO, CTO and CISO.

"And You Must Actually Enforce that Policy."

Clearly.

"Encrypt Everything."

Obviously, though encryption is not the only step organisations should take.

"Regardless of Industry, Implement a Data Loss Prevention Strategy."

OMG1: yes, yes, yes – obviously.

"Have a Remediation Plan in Place."

OMG 2: yes, yes, yes – obviously.

"Conduct Regular Audits for Vulnerabilities."

Any CIO, CISO and chief auditor (and external auditor) who fails to keep "management" aware of threats and the steps they've taken to address them should be fired. Boards of directors that fail to ask questions about digital vulnerability should be replaced. *Information Management* quotes Krishna Narayanaswamy:

> *"For CIOs who haven't performed an assessment of cloud usage in their environment, there's no scarier question than 'How are we using the cloud today?'"*

This is old news. *All* applications and databases are at risk. Stop blaming cloud hosting, which in most cases is much safer than internally hosted applications and databases (Chai, 2022):

> *"Change Passwords Often."*

I don't know how to say *"yes, obviously"* any differently.

"Employ Two-Factor Authentication."

See above. I am out of affirmatives.

> *"Maintain an Open Dialogue with the C-Suite to Discuss Current Policy and Protocols."*

In every single conversation I've had in the past five years and in all the data we've collected over the same period, I can assure you that "awareness" of cyber risk is high. In fact, in all my conversations with executives, it's the easiest sell I've ever experienced. Why? Executives don't want egg on their faces, they don't want to devalue their companies, they don't want to disappoint their customers, don't want to anger their investors and, if they run public companies, don't want to scare their shareholders. Most of all, they loathe looking uninformed and incompetent – because they could lose their lucrative corporate positions. Wrong reasons? Obviously.

"Educate Your Employees on Why This All Matters."

(Sarcastically) probably a good idea (as it was in the twentieth century and ever since).

Digital security is a rapidly growing problem. The digital crime wave is here. Risk will grow as everything becomes increasingly digital and connected. This is no different, by the way, than when the number of automobile accidents increased when more cars took to the road. The relationship between ubiquity and risk is well known. Security breaches and all flavours of cyberwarfare increase as the world becomes increasingly digital. Our response to these risks is always incomplete. Just as air bags came late to reduce the number of fatalities, we're late to reduce cyber risk.

The essential truth, however, is disturbing and, for many segments of our population, unacceptable. Everyone must come to grips with the reality that cyber risk cannot be eliminated and that we'll all face risks, breaches, crimes and perhaps even wars attributable to digital hacking of one kind or another. It's naïve for us to believe that this threat will ever disappear. The best we can do is try to reduce the likelihood of digital mischief and crime, and plan for the *inevitable* management of the impact that mischief and crime will have on our lives, our companies and our way of life. Add cyber risk to the list of "manageable-but-never-solvable" problems – like global warming, pandemics and terrorism.

Westar (2022) presents a list of traditional best practices:

1. *Train employees in security principles.*
2. *Protect information, computers and networks from viruses, spyware and other malicious code.*
3. *Provide firewall security for your Internet connection.*
4. *Download and install software updates for your operating systems and applications as they become available.*
5. *Make backup copies of important business data and information.*
6. *Control physical access to your computers and network components.*
7. *Secure your Wi-Fi networks.*
8. *Require individual user accounts for each employee.*
9. *Limit employee access to data and information, and limit authority to install software.*
10. *Regularly change passwords.*

Alton (2020) offers another list customised for small businesses:

1. *Cloud security.*
2. *Network security.*
3. *VPNs and firewalls.*
4. *Updates and upgrades.*
5. *Data backups.*
6. *Segmented and limited access.*
7. *Employee training.*
8. *Security culture.*

There's nothing wrong with these lists. In fact, you need to follow them for no other reason than to satisfy your auditors and some partners that need to assess your ability to deal with attacks. But even if you take all the steps, don't expect cyberattacks to disappear. Many of them are just for show.

THE COUNTERINTUITIVE PLAY (OR AT LEAST SOMETHING TO THINK ABOUT)

Now, let's have a really tough conversation.

Remember *SolarWinds* (Oladimeji and Kerner, 2022). I've already mentioned it, but all you probably remember – now that I've jogged your memory – is that it's linked to some kind of cyberattack, but you can't explain exactly what happened, what was hacked or what happened after the attack. It was only a couple of years ago, right? Or was it more recent? Maybe longer. Do you know what actually happened? Were the Russians involved? What did they do? Was *Microsoft* involved? What did *they* do? Do you know if the US Government still uses *SolarWinds* software?

CONSEQUENCES?

I ask these questions to obviously make the point that cyberattacks – even big ones like *SolarWinds* – are quickly forgotten, and that the consequences are generally "small". Was Russia punished for the attack? How? Were *SolarWinds* and *Microsoft* punished? Did they lose all of their customers? Did they pay massive fines? Was everyone involved fired on the spot – or ever?

All everyone talks about – including me – is how cyberattacks are increasing and that companies (and government agencies) need to spend more money on cybersecurity. Yes, the number and severity of cyberattacks is increasing: nothing new here. *SolarWinds* reported that it spent about $19 million since the attack to fix the problems that enabled the breach (Satter, 2021). (*SolarWinds'* annual revenue is about $740 million.) The insurance industry was also "happy" with the financial impact of the attack (Shah, 2021):

> *"While the SolarWinds hack is proving to be a devastating cyberattack from a national security perspective, the attack did not evolve into a cyber catastrophe for the insurance market."*

What about those affected by the breach? What will *they* spend (Ratnam, 2021):

> *"American businesses and government agencies could be spending upward of $100 billion over many months to contain and fix the damage from the Russian hack against the SolarWinds software used by so many Fortune 500 companies and U.S. government departments."*

Could these companies have prevented the breach? No. Are they responsible for the clean-up? Will *SolarWinds* help them pay for the clean-up? What do you think?

THE REAL COST OF BREACHES

The real cost of a breach comprises at least five elements, which can all be quantified:

1. The cost to fix what led to the breach and its impact.
2. The reputational risk to the breached company and subsequent loss of revenue and a decline of valuation.
3. Regulatory fines (measured as a percentage of revenue).
4. The cost to defend and settle class action lawsuits.
5. The insurance offset.

The costs to fix what led to breaches are all over the place. Some companies spend a few million dollars while others spend tens of millions. As suggested above, *SolarWinds* reported that it spent about $19 million since the attack to fix the problems that enabled the breach against an annual revenue of about $740 million. The average cost of a data breach in 2020 was about $3.8 million (according to the *Ponemon Institute's* Cost of a Data Breach Report, available at https://www.ibm.com/downloads/cas/3R8N1DZJ).

Reputational risks are more intriguing. Short-term losses – as you would expect – can be significant, but long-term risks are much less so. *Comparitech* suggests that breaches do not necessarily result in collapsing stock prices (Comparitech, 2021):

> *"The size of a breach does not directly correlate to bigger drops in stock prices ... companies that experienced a breach actually performed better in the six months after (the breach) ..."*

Intriguing for sure.

Fines?

Home Depot's annual revenue in 2022 was over $150 billion. The fine for breaches over time was $200 million (Hill, 2022). You'll find that, generally, fines represent a small percentage of revenue. Fines can also be levied outside the USA, but here too the numbers are, well, also intriguing. Still not convinced (Swinhoe, 2022)?

> *"Marriott International was initially fined £99 million [~$124 million] after payment information, names, addresses, phone numbers, email addresses and passport numbers of up to 500 million customers were compromised. The source . . . Marriott's Starwood subsidiary . . . (but) the final penalty was far smaller. The hotel chain was actually only made to pay £18.4million [~$23.7 million] after over a year's delay . . ."*

Marriot International's revenue in 2021 was almost $14B.

The cost to defend and settle class action lawsuits is highly variable but can easily run into the tens of millions – or not, depending on the number and validity of the suits. As they say, it all depends, and most companies that receive large fines have teams of lawyers to appeal fine decisions and often "negotiate" much smaller amounts.

Insurance (Embroker Team, 2022)?

> *"Given the enormous potential cost of a data breach, most businesses should consider investing in a cyber insurance policy with a data breach inclusion. The right cyber insurance policy will allow you to*

transfer all data breach-related risks and costs to your insurer in return for a monthly fee or premium."

So how bad are breaches, really? Do you think that part of the reason why cybersecurity is underfunded is because of liability? Do breaches have manageable consequences? Is a breach a game-changer for a company? Not usually (and hardly ever).

Look what happens when a company's database is breached. The company must reveal the breach in a designated period of time. Millions of records, including addresses, phone numbers and credit card numbers, are sold to the highest bidder. Customers are billed for things they never bought (though don't have to pay for them). While the company's reputation suffers somewhat and likely not long-term – because breaches are so commonplace – impact to their reputation is minimal and short-lived. The auditors then arrive to inspect everything and declare that the company did its best (or not) to prevent the breach. Sometimes, there's a fine, even a large one, but often there's not, and the fines are generally a tiny percentage of annual revenue (and frequently negotiated much lower).

You can decide, but if I'm at the helm and I know that I'll have to pay a fine of less than 1 per cent of my revenue for a major breach, that my customers will return and the price of my stock will recover, I'm not sure how obsessed I'd be – or if I'd be obsessed at all – with cybersecurity spending. While I cannot believe I'm even asking this question, how much should I really spend when I know the hit to my public image (and pocketbook) will be temporary? If I also know that no matter how much I spend I'm still vulnerable to attack, how much should I spend?

Listen to what *Deloitte* says about the relationship between cybersecurity funding and impact (Bobrow, 2022):

"The most striking conclusion in Deloitte's report is that 'money alone is probably not the answer, as higher cybersecurity spending did not necessarily translate into a higher maturity level' … there was not a strong correlation between those that spent a lot and the maturity ratings achieved."

Is underspending an acknowledgement that this is an unsolvable problem with manageable consequences? If you satisfy the auditors, the Board and the executive team, but swim upstream when everyone calls for massive new spending, is that "enough"? Does that even make sense?

Maybe the play is to absolutely respect the threat, adopt every auditor-approved best practice, but don't overspend on cybersecurity. You will eventually be breached, hacked and blamed. So what? Spend "just enough" to keep everyone happy? The consequences of "just enough" spending maybe aren't great enough to justify massive investments. Or maybe they are. There are good "optics" around new – and well-publicised – cybersecurity spending.

I realise this is an unconventional approach to cybersecurity – to put it mildly. Yes, the number and severity of cyberattacks is growing. But can you prevent them? Can you manage them?

Maybe the best you can do is reduce the number and severity of cyber-attacks. Perhaps breach management is where you should focus your efforts. But given the consequences of poor or even "average" cybersecurity investments – remember the *Deloitte* study – you should spend what you need to spend to be compliant. The worst thing you can do is adopt – and expect – a zero-tolerance policy and fund it massively and endlessly. There just isn't enough money on the planet to eliminate the possibility of cyberattacks. But there are people watching you. Make sure they're happy, pay the fines (post-negotiation), be patient, settle the lawsuits and buy insurance.

CYBERSECURITY PLAYS

The number and severity of cyberattacks will increase. All companies are vulnerable and will continue to be no matter how much they invest in cybersecurity.

It's important to embrace industry best practices at least "for show". You must embrace the best practices required of your industry regardless of how effective they might be in securing your networks, databases and applications. You must satisfy your auditors and partners.

You should understand that the consequences of breaches and other attacks are not as impactful as they might be. Consequently, companies – maybe yours – may underinvest in cybersecurity with some level of impunity.

Remember Deloitte concludes that "money alone is probably not the answer," as higher cybersecurity spending did not necessarily translate into a higher maturity level . . . "measured on a per FTE basis, as a percentage of the IT budget, or as a share of revenue, the surveyed companies spent a wide range of their budgets on cyber-security. But there was not a strong correlation between those that spent a lot and the maturity ratings achieved."

What's enough?

Cyberwarfare management is as important as cybersecurity investments.

CHAPTER 6

IGNORE REGULATORY POLICY AT YOUR OWN RISK

CHAPTER SUMMARY

- *Technology regulatory policy directly affects your company.*
- *Tracking regulatory policy trends is necessary – another core competency.*
- *Policy areas include privacy and surveillance, Internet for All, surveillance, misinformation, anti-trust, cybersecurity, AI and machine learning, cryptocurrency, fraud and compliance.*
- *Proactive is better than reactive: technology lobbying is necessary.*

THE POLICY PRIORITY

Regulatory policy is everywhere. Some focuses on the structure of the technology industry – like monopolies – and some focuses on specific issues – like privacy. Some policies focus on infrastructure – like Internet for All – and some on specific technologies – like AI and machine learning. You should see policy as a threat and an opportunity to influence policy. Sitting on the sidelines is not an option.

There are at least nine policy areas that might dramatically impact your business. You must track them to assess their potential impact on your business. Some of them will directly impact your business model and some will impact it indirectly. It's up to you to identify and track these policies, as suggested in Figure 16.

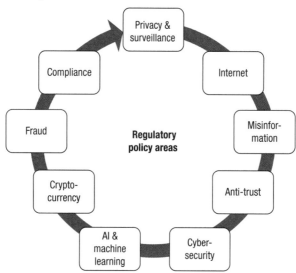

Figure 16 Regulatory policy areas

PRIVACY AND SURVEILLANCE

The amazing truth about the obvious and growing loss of privacy is how unconcerned everyone is – which is great news for companies that make their living listening. Technologists started "snooping" around servers, desktops and databases years ago to understand the status of hardware and software and how they should be managed. Enterprise snooping is still a best practice. But snooping is now central to entire national and global business models, and has emerged with a scary name: surveillance capitalism (Wikipedia, 2022). No one predicted how pervasive snooping would become. No one predicted just how much *profit* snooping would generate, and no one predicted how entire populations would essentially shrug their shoulders about how they're stalked each and every day – to make someone else – *you?* – money.

Lots of us have described how digital surveillance is now pervasive. When surveillance stopped at the data centre, all was well. But the extension of snooping into surveillance to anyone with a digital device is relatively new. It's worth saying again: every time we blog, tweet, post, rideshare, order from *Amazon*, rent from *Airbnb* – or anything that leaves a digital trail – we feed what Shoshana Zuboff (Wikipedia, 2022) calls "surveillance capitalism", which is:

> *"The monetization of data captured through monitoring people's movements and behaviors online and in the physical world, and which is summarized in the New York Times. Countless digital systems now track where we are, where we go, what we eat, what we think, who we like, who we love, where we bank, what we know and who we hate – among lots of other things they know all too well because we remind them over and over again (Zuboff, 2019)."*

On Sunday, 26 January 2020, in a special section titled "One Nation, Tracked", *The New York Times* presented some frightening stories (Thompson and Warzel, 2021):

- *"12 Million Phones, One Dataset, Zero Privacy"*
- *"How to Track the President"*
- *"Eyes on the Capital"*
- *"How Your Phone Betrays Democracy"*
- *"Where Even the Children Are Being Tracked"*
- *"Total Surveillance is Not What America Signed Up For"*

Among other startling revelations, *The New York Times* feature describes just how easy it is to track and predict everyone's behaviour. As part of the ongoing *"Privacy Project", The Times* analyses every aspect of surveillance. While Americans say they're concerned about privacy, they continue to share the most intimate details of their personal lives – not to mention their locations – on social media. They use *Waze, Amazon, Uber, Facebook, Lyft, Google Search, Instagram, Open Table, Trip Advisor, WhatsApp, Google Maps, Skype, Airbnb, eBay* and *Pinterest* more than ever. They "know" about surveillance but only offer "concern" as a response, just like "environmentalists" who continue to drink water from plastic bottles.

So, where does this go – and why might it matter to you? California has taken a step – long after the Europeans took an important one – to control the use of personal data. But there's a conundrum. If everyone denied their personal data to the sites and companies that monetise it, then lots of business models would collapse – unless, of course, the same sites and companies charged for their services. How many Americans, for example, would pay hundreds of dollars a year (or much more) to search the web – or send and receive email? How many would use *Uber* if the cost per ride doubled or tripled (and, during surges, quadrupled)?

The business models that drive huge amounts of the economy are based upon volunteered data, even if the volunteers have no idea how generous they are. Will the California Privacy Act spread across the USA? What happens if a significant number of Americans stop sharing their data? Which companies would suffer the most? *Would your company suffer?* How would you respond?

If Americans "opt out", will they have to pay (or pay extra) for the service the vendors provide? Where's the balance? Can the needle be threaded? You need to track this closely.

Transparency regulations are under consideration. The larger surveillance challenge will be addressed when the cost rises to levels that cannot be ignored, or to a level where the media declares privacy as a cause célèbre, which itself is a commentary about privacy. Said a little differently, privacy is now an essential component of twenty-first century business models and processes and a huge generator of profitable revenue. If that's the case, and you make money from surveillance data, are you safe?

Profitable revenue, in turn, generates social, economic and political power which can be leveraged to manipulate privacy. If this process continues to evolve, surveillance will become a component of lots of digital business models, and therefore a direct path to profitability (while privacy becomes a threat – not to our personal freedoms – but to profitability). At that point, even the media cannot derail surveillance. Or it goes the other (unlikely) way, and Americans accept the real cost of privacy. Regardless of speculation, you need to track these trends closely.

While the USA does not have a national data privacy policy, some US states are moving closer to GDPR-like privacy policies. What if everyone was given the right to opt out of the collection and distribution of personal data without losing privileged services or paying higher rates or extra fees? Media companies or ISPs that collect and sell personal data would be severely impacted if the USA enacted a GDPR.

Pay attention.

INTERNET FOR ALL

Some countries have already defined "the internet" as a public utility and have crafted "regulations" around access, provisioning and privacy. In the USA, under the Obama administration, net neutrality tilted toward public utility status, while under the Trump administration, tilting went in the other direction. The Biden administration is tilting back toward net neutrality. Who knows what future administrations will do? This is about the power that ISPs are given to control access to the internet. Should they, for example, have fewer or more restrictions regarding their pricing schemes to content providers?

The major assumption of those against net neutrality is that deregulation will encourage innovation since commercial ISPs can charge certain customers more money than others (in exchange for most-favoured provisioning). The "extra" money can be ploughed back into internet infrastructure projects that benefit everyone. The proponents of net neutrality argue that, without regulation in some form, there will be abuses of access, distribution and privacy. What are the issues? Some of the major ones include the control of data, digital rights, digital freedoms, slow-loading, competition, innovation, standards, pseudo-services and privacy, among others. But at the end of the day, it's about control and the regulatory oversight necessary to enable consumer *and* corporate rights and freedoms.

If your company relies upon the internet or makes money as an ISP or a content provider, policy is of enormous importance to your business model and the processes it enables. Failing to track the net neutrality pendulum – and eventual outcome – is a major mistake.

MISINFORMATION AND DISINFORMATION

There are real/fake information countermeasures under consideration you should track. An obvious one that comes to mind is real-time digital fact-checking. When someone says something that is scientifically or empirically wrong, should it be exposed with multiple sources that reject the assertion? The process could be automated with smart fact-checkers continuously trolling the web for lies – regardless of the source. Some have suggested "delays" of live broadcasts to check the facts before airing statements that may or may not be true. Live streaming has complicated the veracity of "facts", since not everything is as it seems, as we've learned over decades of mass media experience. Are there delay and due diligence measures under consideration?

Regulation would enable the exposure of myths and lies about issues like "evolution" with longstanding scientific knowledge, and even myths about the shape of the earth. (If we have to argue about overwhelming scientific evidence, then we have a much larger problem.)

If your strategy, business model and business processes rely upon the creation and distribution of misinformation or disinformation, you need to track regulatory trends that will impact your effectiveness. (You might also want to look yourself in the mirror.)

Calls for regulation here are growing. The problems of course – again – are the business models that depend upon misinformation, such as public and private media that wins by attracting as many participants as possible. The regulatory agenda here is complex, since in the USA it involves the First Amendment to the US Constitution. That said, there's a floor upon which "free speech" builds. Hate websites weaken the foundation. Does the exploitation of media access and the manipulation of content for political advantage require regulation? Does the deliberate dissemination of false content over public networks require regulation? Is the re-categorisation of technology companies as media companies imminent?

If you make money from misinformation or disinformation (or fighting them), these questions – and possible regulatory fallout – are important.

ANTI-TRUST

De facto monopolies are everywhere. Cloud delivery, internet search, social media, operating system and rideshare markets are monopolies. It's no secret that monopolies constrain innovation. Anti-trust policies – which come and go – can affect the structure of many industries.

David Wessel (2018), writing in the *Harvard Business Review,* is straightforward:

> *"Despite their undeniable popularity, Apple, Amazon, Google, and Facebook are drawing increasing scrutiny from economists, legal scholars, politicians, and policy wonks, who accuse these firms of using their size and strength to crush potential competitors. Technology giants pose unique challenges, but they also represent just one piece of a broader story: a troubling phenomenon of too little competition throughout the U.S. economy."*

If your vested interests are spread across the innovation and entrepreneurialism worlds, this is a troubling trend. Tracking trends here is essential if you're a technology monopolist, oligarch or entrepreneur.

CYBERSECURITY

The US digital infrastructure is leaky, to put it mildly. Just as dangerous, the digital infrastructure and the most popular applications – like social media – are vulnerable to manipulation by terrorists, hackers, adversaries, and human and software bots (see Chapter 5 for more detail). Will new regulations require investments to protect infrastructures, databases and applications? This could cost you money. Are you watching?

According to the *US Department of Homeland Security* (DHS, 2018), the threats are everywhere and growing. *DHS* believes that the USA should:

> *"Strengthen our efforts as part of the law enforcement community to pursue, counter, reduce, and disrupt illicit cyber activity by leveraging, In particular, our specialized expertise and capabilities to target financial and transborder cybercrimes . . . the transnational and cross-jurisdictional nature of cyberspace, as well as the sheer size of the challenge, requires closer collaboration with other federal, state, local, and international law enforcement partners."*

If you do business with the government – which thousands of companies do – you must track regulatory trends here. There are all sorts of regulatory steps the US government may take.

Whether you do business with the USA or other governments or not, it may become increasingly difficult to pass cybersecurity audits which today include capabilities in network, data, operations, systems and physical security. Might this list be expanded to include, for example, reference to specific tools and technologies? Or access to – and the security of – personal data? What might this cost? Can you do it internally or should you outsource it? Your business model and the liabilities connected with your industry will determine which way you go.

ARTIFICIAL INTELLIGENCE AND MACHINE LEARNING

AI and machine learning are powerful problem solvers (see Chapter 4). The design and development of intelligent systems could be affected if regulations around "explainable AI" appear. This would add to the development of intelligent systems and "expose" the way applications make decisions. Are you in these businesses? Will requirements around explainable AI emerge? Will policies emerge that impact your business?

In addition to regulations around explainable AI are regulations around anything autonomous. There might also be regulations around displacements that affect the companies reducing the workforce in certain industries. Regulatory possibilities connected with AI and machine learning are everywhere. Stay tuned.

CRYPTOCURRENCY

Most people who buy a house or a car, or buy things on *Amazon*, never think about "paying" with cryptocurrency. Most people have no idea how many cryptocurrencies there are (over 1,000), though a lot of people have heard about Bitcoin. Very few people realise that cryptocurrency is simultaneously a currency, an investment and a technology: you can buy a house with cryptocurrency, speculate with some of your retirement money in cryptocurrency (and eventually invest in cryptocurrency ETFs) and invest in cryptocurrency's underlying technology (blockchain). But since cryptocurrency is simultaneously a currency, an investment and a technology, there are regulatory possibilities that affect all three aspects of cryptocurrency. What should you know about cryptocurrency?

- Identity theft is essentially impossible with cryptocurrency.
- It's potentially nefarious: money laundering, among other transactions, is easy.
- It's available and immediate.
- More and more businesses will *eventually* accept it.
- It's volatile: the value of Bitcoin and Ethereum, for example, have swung wildly over the past couple of years.

Will more companies accept and trade cryptocurrency? Will more investors – like *Fidelity* (which) enable(s) investors to participate in the cryptocurrency market via ETFs and other investment vehicles (Franck, 2021) – provide cryptocurrency investment opportunities?

Look what the US is doing:

"Under the new rules, cryptocurrency exchanges are regarded as brokers and must comply with relevant . . . reporting and record-keeping obligations . . . President Biden issued an executive order detailing plans to introduce a cryptocurrency regulatory framework. The order involved 6 digital asset priorities: consumer and investor protection, the promotion of financial stability, action against illicit finance, US global financial leadership, financial inclusion, and responsible innovation."

You can see how wide and deep regulatory policy can go. Are you affected by cryptocurrency policy? (Assuming it has teeth, of course.)

Note also that regulations and regulatory possibilities differ around the world where, for example, some countries have prohibited, restricted, approved cryptocurrency assets; many countries are "wait and see". If you're global, you need to track regulatory possibilities around the world.

FRAUD

Regulatory policy around fraud is changing. It's also already voluminous (FDIC, 2022). Fraud policy is internal and external. Internally, you need a clear fraud policy that removes any and all ambiguity about how to define and address fraud.

Externally, you need to comply with laws and regulations around fraud. The *US FBI* can help with the (FBI, 2022):

- *"Falsification of financial information.*
- *"Self-dealing by corporate insiders.*
- *"Kickbacks.*
- *"Money laundering.*
- *"Securities and commodities fraud.*
- *"Mortgage and financial institution fraud.*
- *"Intellectual property theft."*

Internal corporate fraud policies should include the following (Deloitte, 2022):

- *"An explicit definition of actions that are deemed to be fraudulent.*
- *"Allocation of responsibilities for the overall management of fraud.*
- *"A statement that all appropriate measures to deter fraud will be taken.*
- *"The formal procedures which employees should follow if a fraud is suspected.*
- *"Notification that all instances of suspected fraud will be investigated and reported to the appropriate authorities.*
- *"An unequivocal statement that all fraud offenders will be prosecuted and that the police will be assisted in any investigation that is required.*
- *"A statement that all efforts will be made to recover wrongfully obtained assets from fraudsters.*
- *"Encouragement to employees to report any suspicion of fraud.*
- *"The steps to be taken in the event a fraud is discovered and who is responsible for taking action."*

Remember that "fraud audits" are not the same as "fraud examinations" (Carmichael, 2018):

> *"It is not that the fraud examiner and auditor perform similar services, or have equivalent responsibility for fraud detection; the services are distinctly different, and are planned and performed to accomplish unique purposes. Rather, both have a responsibility to detect fraud, and the differences in the nature of that responsibility do not provide an excuse for an auditor's failure to obtain reasonable assurance of detecting a material misstatement due to fraud."*

Will this distinction hold?

Fraud is included here because transaction processing is increasingly digital which means that authentication, bot attacks, disinformation, identity fraud, payment fraud, money laundering, spam management – you name it – are now in play – and those who regulate "digital" are way behind the adoption of digital transaction processing. It's also included here because regulation is already here (Wilson, Sonsini, Goodrich and Rosati, 2019) and will definitely evolve over time.

The regulation of payment systems, digital asset management, data rights, data governance, electronic banking and other areas related to fraud will change as the world goes full-digital.

COMPLIANCE

There are frameworks that define compliance requirements (Tozzi, 2021):

"The General Data Protection Regulation (is the) European Union data protection regulation.

"The California Consumer Privacy Act is currently America's most farreaching consumer privacy and security law.

"The Payment Card Industry Data Security Standard is a standard developed by credit card companies.

"The National Institute of Standards and Technology (is a) cybersecurity framework.

"The Health Insurance Portability and Accountability Act . . . a (US) regulatory compliance framework.

"Sarbanes-Oxley Act . . . introduced in the US . . . to combat corporate fraud."

There are also software tools that track and satisfy compliance requirements – lots of them (Brooks, 2020). Some are general tools – like technology auditing tools – and some are applicable to specific industries.

You need to track compliance requirements as well as the tools that help you comply. This is a core competency.

ADDITIONAL REGULATORY TRENDS

There are additional areas you might want to track, including innovation and talent.

Regarding *innovation,* the US ranks around 25th in the world in R&D tax credits. *Information Technology and Innovation Foundation* (ITIF) Senior Fellow Joe Kennedy (2018) tells us that:

> *"Germany, the UK and China are sweetening the pot, while* the US slides." According to Kennedy, *'The United States needs to follow the international trend. The (ITIF) has called for increasing the tax credit's Alternative Simplified Credit to at least 20% from its current rate of 14%.'"*

Ideally, R&D (and other) credits are separated from overall tax policy and not negotiated as a "trade-off" among unrelated issues. Since tax credits are, well, credits, such proposals should receive bipartisan support; and who wants to campaign for office as an enemy of innovation?

Regarding technology talent, reporter Rani Molla (2019) succinctly described how the immigration barriers the Trump Administration imposed made it increasingly difficult for skilled workers to come to the US – which, regardless of your political party – just makes no sense.

LOBBYING

I assume you're "investing" in politicians, legislation, associations, lobbying groups – you name it – to achieve the regulatory and policy results that make you money. Crass? You bet, but that's what your shareholders and stakeholders expect you to do: play by the rules to change the rules.

Regardless of how you feel about the lobbying profession or the role that lobbying plays in the larger political system, lobbying is a real activity that requires a team, a budget, its own strategy, model and processes. There's lots of help out there. But remember that you're the brains, not the brawn.

There are at least two types of lobbying (Duke Health, 2022):

"Direct Lobbying: Any attempt to influence legislation through communication with: (i) Any member or employee of a legislative body, or (ii) any government official or employee (other than a member or employee of a legislative body) who may participate in the formulation of the legislation, but only if the principal purpose of the communication is to influence legislation.

"Grassroots Lobbying: An attempt to influence legislation through an attempt to affect the opinions of the general public or any segment of the public."

You should play both ends.

Aggressively.

REGULATORY POLICY PLAYS

You should see policy as a threat and an opportunity to influence regulations.

Policy areas include privacy and surveillance, Internet for All, surveillance, mis-information, anti-trust, cybersecurity, AI and machine learning, cryptocurrency, fraud and compliance, among others.

"Invest" in politicians, legislation, associations, lobbying groups to achieve the regulatory and policy results that make you money: play by the rules to change the rules by direct and grassroots lobbying.

CHAPTER 7

LEAD, MANAGE AND GOVERN THE RIGHT GAME

CHAPTER SUMMARY

- *There are ongoing leadership and management challenges: you cannot win every game.*
- *Core competencies must be reclaimed; "internal consultants" can replace the usual consultant suspects.*
- *Too many "Chiefs" create unnecessary silos – and too many complications.*
- *Hierarchical management structures make more sense than flat ones, especially for remote work.*
- *Emotions must be controlled.*
- *Enterprise governance is key.*

LEADERSHIP AND MANAGEMENT CHALLENGES

There are over 50,000 leadership books for sale on *Amazon*. There are hundreds of executive leadership programmes and thousands of leadership courses. Leadership "Master Classes" are all the rage from celebrities (who, in many cases, have never actually led anything).

With all this guidance, why are there still so many failed leaders? How many companies suffer bad management? At the end of the day, most "management" is *reactive* to markets, competition and crises. It's not *proactive.* Reactive management is "easier" than management that requires true creative strategising and decision making based on data, experience, forecasting and best practices. Checkers *is* easier than chess, and no one seems to care when the game abruptly ends in another tie. But chess is complicated, which is why it's so challenging – and only played by a small subset of managers. Perhaps most importantly, leadership and management fail to focus on strategic technology.

Let's stipulate that leadership and management challenges have been with us for decades. As we discuss business-technology leadership, management, organisation and structure, we must acknowledge that there are no perfect leaders, no perfect plays and no perfect game plan. But you should also know that your competition has the same challenges.

RECLAIM CORE COMPETENCIES WITH "INTERNAL CONSULTANTS"

Now that we've stipulated the inevitability of leadership and management challenges, let's turn to some steps that can reduce the number and severity of the challenges. Let's start with brains versus brawn and the leadership and management implications of mistaken identity.

I've argued about core competencies throughout this playbook. I've argued that most companies already outsource way too many activities to consultants who have no special claim on the knowledge and expertise they sell. *McKinsey*, *Accenture*, *Cap Gemini* – and lots of other consultancies – do a decent job diagnosing and solving operational technology problems. But "decent" is relative: *Gartner* reminds us that 75 per cent of all ERP projects fail – even when high-profile (and high-priced) consultants "help". In fact, big software project failure is pervasive. Almost everyone in the industry knows that software projects fail far more often than they succeed.

Strategic technology?

They all want to play, but very few can do it as well as you should.

The issue – internal versus external consulting – persists (Consultancy-me, 2022). There are endless lists of strengths and weaknesses of each kind of consulting (9Lenses, 2022). Some are extremely well described (Authenticity Consulting, 2020). That said, if a company wants to leverage digital technology to improve, automate, or replace its business processes and whole business models, it must understand and model its own processes, its own business model and the technologies that enable process improvement.

Where should you draw the line? How much about a company do those who manage it already know? (A lot.) Should you trust strangers? (No.) How much will be lost in translation? (Tons.) Or should you just do it yourself? (Yes.) Let's discuss how this gets done with "internal consultants", which should be designated as such in your company.

The strengths of internal consultants usually revolve around knowledge of company processes – and all things strategic. This is where the calculation of relative strengths and weaknesses occurs. Can we argue that external consultants know more about the strategy of their clients than the clients themselves? External consultants will reflexively say *"Yes, of course we do!"* But they don't, shouldn't and never have.

Digital leverage requires an integrated understanding of your company's strategic strengths, weaknesses and intentions, and an understanding of the technologies necessary for it to win. Leverage also requires an intimate understanding of a company's language, ways of working, culture and the politics that explain what's possible. External consultants simply cannot know these things unless they move in and stay for a long while (which they'd love to do). More broadly – and this is the key point – "digital" is now the primary competitive advantage you exert on your competition. The design of a digital strategy simply cannot be trusted to consultants. There's nothing more "core" than competency in this area.

What if you developed a team of in-house consultants to help you identify, model and solve your strategic technology problems? What if these teams functioned much the same way that *McKinsey*, *BCG* and *Bain* function? What if they also provided a level of candour that external consultants – for fear of losing the engagement – never provide? These teams could be composed of employees that rotate in and out of the consulting group, which could be seen – and rewarded – as a prestigious assignment. There are lots of ways to formally structure and organise this team and lots of ways to recruit, grow and reward internal consultants.

The play is clear: rethink the role external consultants play at your company, and then consider how an internal team might accelerate success.

Brains versus brawn? You bet.

REDUCE THE # OF CHIEFS

I've been a "chief" several times in my career and while the title is nice, it often didn't mean very much to the organisations I've led. Of course, this may be attributable to my own skills and competencies, but it may also be attributable to something else: the falsely purposeful need to centralise expertise and authority in someone supremely responsible and accountable for achieving specific results. Put more simply, we love leaders (and especially leadership titles) because we can turn our lonely eyes to someone who can just make us feel better (and someone we can blame when things go wrong).

I've recently seen calls for chief digital marketing officers, chief data officers, chief analytics officers, chief social media officers, chief content officers, chief transformation officers, chief cloud officers and chief digital strategy officers, among lots of other chiefs, including of course the existing ones, like CIOs, CTOs and CISOs – *and their deputies.* Is there room for all these chiefs? Who's authorising all these empires?

Specialisation in a converging world is misguided. The number of chiefs you have explains your level of organisational complexity: the more chiefs, the more complex your business structures, rules and processes. Chiefs increase organisation autonomy, atrophy and dysfunction. The more you have, the more confusion and conflict you will experience.

Lots of chiefs also challenge your governance structures and processes (see below for more on enterprise governance). Let's assume you have ten technology chiefs with their own missions, teams and budgets. You assume they will coordinate and cooperate, but general incentive structures and competitive instincts make it impossible for chiefs to love one another – or always stay in their mission swim lanes. Chief data officers will intrude upon chief digital marketing officers – who both need chief cloud officers – while the CISO tells them all what they can and cannot do (with oversight from the chief transformation officer). How is organisational power distributed among the chiefs?

Which chief decides which chief should be chief?

Instead of technology chiefs of one kind or another, you should find fewer chiefs that operate at a higher level of abstraction. Their missions are broader and therefore less invasive of existing business rules, processes and models. They constitute a smaller number of filters through which change can occur which enables speed and agility.

But even this approach – fewer chiefs – still assumes the intrinsic value of "chiefs". What if there was another way to optimise digital technology? What if "digital" became a way of life?

The less-enterprise-chiefs approach requires a different kind of investment. At first glance, it appears to take longer and cost more, but compared to multiple dysfunctional enterprise chiefdoms, it's much cheaper and more productive.

The first step is a general education across the leadership about the trends and capabilities of digital technology. No single team – or even groups of teams – should exclusively own and dispense this knowledge. It's not possible or desirable for knowledge that enables business-technology optimisation to exist in silos: it's the combination of subject matter expertise *and* digital technology that identifies opportunities. Everyone should understand digital technologies, trends and trajectories, and how business rules, processes and whole business models can be transformed for profitable advantage.

The next step is the creation of a knowledge repository run by a corporate "digital librarian", an internal *Google* search engine capable of answering questions about the intersection of company and industry processes and models, and digital technology.

The third step is the creation of mini innovation labs in every business unit informed by the general education and the enterprise repository. Over time, entire business units will become transformation machines.

There are no convoluted governance processes and no turf battles across poorly defined chiefdoms in this model. It's a "state's rights" approach to corporate governance, where business units are the states, and the enterprise is the federal government. But let's not go too far with the analogy. The approach does not favour strong governors, just strong mayors.

You get the idea: you don't need any more business-technology chiefs.

ORGANISE HIERARCHICALLY

One of the *Gartner Group's* predictions for technology organisations is flat-out bizarre (Eide, 2021):

> *"By 2024, 30% of corporate teams will be without a boss due to the self-directed and hybrid nature of work."*

I have no problem with management by outcomes-versus-processes, especially in technology, and especially when work is remote. *But the expected outcome had better be clear, or the employee will drift from management's requirements.* There are all sorts of conditions that determine if outcome management works. Clarity, style, timing, documentation, relationships, history, precedent, collaboration, and who knows what, must all be specified, not implied. Specificity here is your friend; ambiguity is your enemy. Some professionals will be good with this. Many will not.

We're always searching for new ways to "manage". All structures are flawed, so, as the argument goes, pick one and live with it. But the pandemic work-at-home challenge has strained even the most (relatively) effective organisations. No one really knows what everyone actually does all day or where they're doing it. No one knows who's listening and no one knows how to evaluate remote performance. Especially vulnerable are companies whose ways of working are verbal, not based on actual documentation. You know the companies – maybe like yours – that don't always document what they're doing, who's doing what and what the performance metrics should be, versus companies that are crystal clear in what they expect specific people to do when, how and with what evidence.

The *"let's not write everything down"* companies have an especially tough time conducting annual performance reviews, which themselves are done from the mountains, the beaches or someone's basement office. You know what I mean. Some companies are not just flat in structure, they're also flat in documentation. Decision-making audit trails – *"who agreed to this?"* – are thin at best, versus companies who would pass post-decision-making audits with exquisite detail around responsibility and accountability.

Some companies rely upon RACI charting to help clarify all this. RACI charting requires companies to clarify project and larger programmatic roles. There are lots of definitions of RACI charts. Here's one (Montgomery and Kumar, 2020) that's clear (the **bold** is mine):

> *"A RACI chart . . . is a diagram that **identifies the key roles and responsibilities of users against major tasks within a project.** RACI charts serve as a visual representation of the functional role played by each person on a project team. **Creating these charts is also an excellent exercise in balancing workload and establishing the decision-maker."***

"RACI" refers to **r**esponsible, **a**ccountable, **c**onsultative and **i**nformation status, that is, who's responsible versus who's just informed. But how many companies do you really know that are fully committed to RACI charting? (There's more about RACI charts in Chapter 8.)

At the core of leadership and management are two general organisational philosophies: mechanistic and organic (Devaney, 2022). You guessed it: mechanistic is the more structured, predictable one. Organic structures are the ones you're more likely to find in start-ups:

> *"Mechanistic structures . . . are known for having narrow spans of control, as well as high centralization, specialization, and formalization . . . as daunting and inflexible as mechanistic structure sounds, the chain of command, whether long or short, is always clear . . . as a company grows, it needs to make sure everyone (and every team) knows what's expected of them.*

> *"Organic structures (also known as "flat" structures) are known for their wide spans of control, decentralization, low specialization, and loose departmentalization . . . this model might have multiple teams answering to one person and taking on projects based on their importance and what the team is capable of — rather than what the team is designed to do . . . this organizational structure is much less formal than mechanistic and takes a bit of an ad-hoc approach to business needs. This can sometimes make the chain of command,*

whether long or short, difficult to decipher. And as a result, leaders might give certain projects the green light more quickly but cause confusion in a project's division of labor."

Each one of these philosophies has variants but the implications are clear. Structured versus unstructured. Top down versus bottom-up – and across. Hierarchical versus flat.

Covid opened the door for alternative ways of working. Employees discovered life–work balance through remote work. Many don't want to return to the commuting grind. They crave flexibility. Due to unfulfilled childcare and leaves-of-absence policies, the USA is a green field for new ways of working. Covid gave them a de facto taste of life in other countries that have more flexible work/leave policies. Professionals like what they tasted. Some companies like it too. It's cheaper than renting all that physical space, right? Gig workers may be the answer versus hiring all those benefit-heavy employees. If healthcare was universal in the USA, we'd see huge shifts in our ways of working.

What does all this have to do with organisational structures?

If present trends continue, the fog of remote performance and account-ability will increase. In academia, for example, *Zoom* – and more general trends toward online education – have transformed "work". Professors teaching only in online degree programs are based everywhere but in their academic headquarters. I know professors who have never been to their campuses. I know administrators who don't even know – or care – where their professors live. Can this be true for sales and marketing profession-als? *No – unless they're managed hierarchically.* Unlike professors, whose performance and accountability swirl around specific, measurable teaching performance metrics (and whose "management" has always been remotely managed), corporate professionals need specific performance metrics measured against a set of changing requirements that must be defined and closely tracked by managers – and the only way to do this is through mechanistic organisational structures.

Put a little differently, do you want your sales, marketing, finance and HR professionals defining and prioritising their work without direction?

I have no idea why any of this is controversial. These days, it's popular to empower and entrust everyone to do the right corporate things. Flat is good. Network structures are good. Teams work well together when man-agement just leaves them alone. Right? As remote work trends expand, companies should contract their management structures. As old school as it sounds, there's gold in popping into an office to check on a project. Assuming offices are virtual, which for a lot of reasons they should be, "checking" needs structure. Checking hates ambiguity. Checking needs evidence. Before the Covid pandemic, we could "see" the evidence face-to-face, but with new work protocols, "seeing" takes on different forms, which is fine so long as there's no confusion about who gets to look and what they're expected to see.

Virtual checking is also possible – and necessary – when there's clarity around roles and responsibilities.

Reject flat; stay hierarchical.

WATCH YOUR EMOTIONS

Major technology investments are often driven by a wide range of emotions. Said a little differently, many technology decisions are based upon feelings. Some good, some bad and some dangerous. But *feelings* – not empirical due diligence – which explains why so many technology investments fail to deliver operational or strategic value.

It's important to understand just how emotional many technology decisions can be. CEOs, CIOs, CTOs and CISOs – and all the other chiefs – are just like everyone else, motivated by biases, fear, hope, ignorance, confusion, denial and stubbornness, among other emotions that can exert more influence than due diligence data when their companies write checks to their favourite vendors, promote the most loyal members of their teams or develop strategies based solely on their judgment and instinct – even when there's tons of empirical evidence suggesting the investments make no sense.

Fear, confusion, optimism, uncertainty, denial and worse are driving some of the most expensive operational and strategic technology decisions a company can make. Skills assessments are often "personal". Very few business-technology decision managers assess the skills and capabilities of their teams objectively. Instead, they make assessments based on relationships, references from friends, direct and indirect experiences and reputations, among other subjective variables. Biased employee appraisals are well documented (Symonds, 2022). Some of the more persistent biases include the "halo effect", the length-of-service bias, the leniency bias, the contrast bias and the "similar-to-me" bias (Julie, 2018), among many others.

The challenge for those who evaluate the performance of technology professionals are the rapidly changing skills/competencies requirements. The list of requirements today includes the ability to optimise cloud computing, analytics, mobile applications, artificial intelligence/machine learning, augmented and virtual reality, blockchain, the Internet of Things, wearables and even cryptocurrency, among other technologies and technology acquisition, deployment and measurement best practices – all of which change every three years. The chances are good that tenured chiefs will not have all the necessary skills and competencies to optimise technology investing, so executives must be brutally honest about the skills gaps among their teams, though very few are. *"Are you serious?"* you might hear someone say, *"I play golf with Charlie every week! Now you want to me replace him?"*

If your company is fraught with biases, fear, hope, confusion, denial and stubbornness – which it is to some extent – what's the solution?

Five steps:

- Step 1 is The first step is *awareness*. It's necessary to acknowledge the role that emotion plays in technology management. If this step is ignored, emotion will rule.

- Step 2 *requires everyone to adhere to due diligence best practices followed by outsiders with no vested personal or financial interests in their analyses.*

- Step 3 *requires due diligence analysts to seek second and third data-driven recommendations* about (especially) large and even small technology investments.

- Step 4 *requires the quantification of all variables* on the due diligence checklist.

- Step 5 – by far the most difficult step – seeks to *modify the corporate, government and personal cultures that allow emotion to play too large a role in technology decision making.*

I can confirm the role that emotion plays in the technology acquisition, management and assessment process. Lots of pressures, too much misinformation, suspicious vendors, uncertainty, lots of political deals, longstanding personal relationships, way too much hope and denial, the need to succeed at all costs – and fail when no one's watching – all favour emotion over empiricism. As a CTO in a Global 100 company, for example, we lived in denial, underinvesting in infrastructure and applications. We "knew" we needed to spend more money shoring things up, but C-suite pressure to keep technology costs as low as possible was relentless.

As a consultant, I've worked with companies who made massive technology investments without nearly enough analysis or evidence to support their decisions. They simply followed the pack – and then wondered why the wheels came off shortly after the projects began. I've watched government agencies manage technology with friends. Many others found it impossible to objectively assess technology teams and sometimes actually generously promoted employees who should have been dismissed. I've witnessed C-suites behave badly about security, rewards, staffing and vendors due to personal relationships with the principals and other inexplicable emotions.

Watch what you feel.
Watch what your colleagues feel.
Watch what your company feels.

GOVERNANCE

All of this rolls up to governance.

Pay very serious attention to the importance of governance, which is about rules, roles, relationships and ways of working. Unless you're unique, you have problems with governance precisely because it deals with rules, roles, relationships and ways of working.

Some simple governance questions:

- Do you have any rules?
- Are the roles of all the members of your team clearly codified?
- Are the relationships among team members and whole teams well-defined?
- Are the ways your company works consistent with the rules, roles and relationships?

Listen to me: ambiguity is always your enemy. The more ambiguity around rules, roles, relationships and ways of working at your company, the less productive you will be. Do you choose to live in states of confusion? Let's unpack this question. We both know that when projects are conceived or when projects launch, there's an inordinate amount of discussion about how Person A will interact with Person B (C, D, E . . .), who should be cc'd on emails (and who shouldn't), who should get invited to meetings (and who shouldn't), who should present (and who shouldn't), who should write the business case (and who shouldn't) and on and on and on. The number of end runs, leaps and secret steps is incalculable. Imagine how the number of steps could be reduced if everyone knew what their job was.

RACI charting is a good start, but much more is required.

Let's look at the *role* of a chief technology officer:

- The chief technology officer (CTO) is responsible for all products and services that touch external customers (internal company customers are supported by a chief information officer [CIO]).

- The CTO is also responsible for the technology vision of the company where new products and services are identified, piloted and developed in response to industry trends, customer requirements and competitive positioning.

- The CTO develops technology strategies to increase revenue and performs ROI analysis principally through the management of technology products, services and pilots. The CTO is also responsible for managing the IP embedded in software products and technology services.

- The CTO has a long-term fiduciary responsibility for aligning business strategy with its technology portfolio and evangelising all things digital throughout – and beyond – the company.

- The CTO interacts with the CEO, all executives and the board.

Ways of working?

- The CTO is a key member of the company's strategic leadership team and works closely with the CEO, product management, sales, business development, consulting, marketing and the executive teams of the company.

- The CTO interfaces internally and externally. Internally, the CTO interacts with sales, product management, consulting, business development and the executive team to assure alignment with current and future technology initiatives.

- The CTO also manages the software engineering function of the company, which includes software architecture and software development: the CTO owns the software product portfolio.

- The CTO also interacts closely with the research team to assure alignment of current and emerging IP with technology and software products and services.

- Externally, the CTO interfaces with technology research and analysis organisations and represents the company at key technology and industry conferences.

Do the specifics matter all that much? No.

What matters is the codification of the role, its internal and external relationships and how it works within the company. The communication of all this – for all positions – constitutes governance, so long as there is a mechanism to enforce governance variants.

Governance only works when it's enforced.

Do you have the stomach to enforce rules, roles, relationships and ways of working? (If you don't, don't bother with governance.) Let's agree that "leadership" is always – shall we say – "challenging". We all know what to do. The challenge is to actually do what's necessary. We've all seen leadership and management lists, steps and best practices on paper that are ignored in the trenches. My job is to tell you what to do. I cannot force you to do what's obvious or necessary.

LEADERSHIP AND MANAGEMENT PLAYS

Remember that leadership and management challenges are everywhere. You cannot win every game, so keep things in perspective.

"Internal consultants" can implement the brains versus brawn directive. Teams of consultants can be formed and anointed to perform many of the tasks traditional consultants perform.

Reduce the number of "chiefs" at your company. Resist the industry's desire to create new functions, budgets and silos. Keep it simple. Remember that specialisation in a converging world is misguided. The number of approved, licensed chiefs you have explains your level of organisational complexity: the more chiefs, the more complex your business structures, rules and processes. Chiefs increase organisation autonomy, atrophy and dysfunction. The more you have, the more confusion and conflict. Organise hierarchically; avoid flat management structures especially as you try to assign and track remote work. Consider RACI charts to remove ambiguity. Fear, confusion, optimism, uncertainty, denial and worse are driving some of the most expensive operational and strategic technology decisions you can make. Try to identify them and minimise their impact. Pay very serious attention to the importance of governance, which is about rules, roles, relationships and ways of working. Remember that ambiguity is your lifelong enemy: the more ambiguity around rules, roles, relationships and ways of working at your company, the less productive you will be. Also remember that governance only works when it's enforced.

CHAPTER 8

INNOVATE LIKE YOUR COMPANY DEPENDS ON IT

CHAPTER SUMMARY

- *Innovation is not commercialisation.*
- *"Pitching" successful innovation/commercialisation projects.*
- *Ideation business cases.*
- *DARPA-like innovation/commercialisation lessons.*
- *Emerging technology and innovation/commercialisation.*
- *Innovation/commercialisation governance.*

INNOVATE FOR COMMERCIAL PURPOSES

Here's the most important takeaway of this chapter: innovate for purpose. You innovate to reduce costs and increase profitable revenue – not because it's fun, or because your mad scientists in the basement have killer ideas just waiting to be freed. The second takeaway? Innovation is not commercialisation. They're different. Innovation enables commercialisation – not the other way around.

There are many different definitions and categories of innovation; scholars and practitioners continue to torture the concept in search of definitions they hope everyone will accept.

Here are three (Wikipedia, 2022):

1. *"Innovation is a many-stage process whereby organisations remodel ideas into new and improved services, products or processes, in order to advance, challenge and separate themselves in their marketplace.*

2. *"Maintaining innovation is the advancement of a product or service based on the known requirements of present customers (e.g., better microprocessors, flat screen televisions).*

3. *"Cumulative innovation improves and extends an already established design. Enhancement occurs in individual pieces, but the core design ideas, and the links between them, remain the same."*

For the purposes of this playbook, we'll define innovation as the matrix in Figure 17.

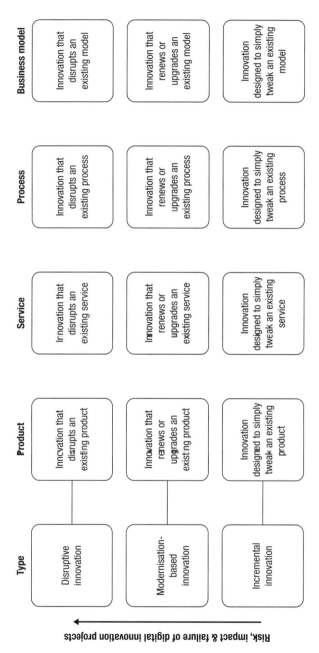

Figure 17 Targets of innovation

There are three distinct kinds of innovation: incremental innovation, innovation that results from modernisation and disruptive innovation. The three kinds are applied to products, services, business processes and whole business models across multiple vertical industries. (If this sounds like the three kinds of digital transformation discussed in Chapter 3, it's because they're cousins.) Most so-called "innovation" is boring. In fact, it's not innovation at all. Most companies love to exaggerate their innovation capabilities and results. Most of them disrupt by accident, context, opportunity – or desperation, which is similar to digital transformation, which, as we discussed in Chapter 3, is seldom transformative.

Amazon started selling books. We met with Jeff Bezos in the 1990s while he was raising money for his eCommerce book site – *which is all he talked about.* Then what? The rest is history. How many companies exploited the Covid-19 pandemic for financial gain? Can you spell *Peloton*? Disruptive innovation is hard, and usually evolves from incremental innovation. Sometimes, it just appears, like *Occulus*. But that's generally not the case. So be careful how you define your innovation projects – unless you're pitching to neophytes. Note also that innovation can hit different markets in different ways. Are you innovating a product? A service? A process? Or an entire business model? Think about *Airbnb*, *VRBO* and *Expedia* and *Kayak*. Did they disrupt a process, a business model or a service? Or all three?

Commercialisation is different. It represents the pivot from innovation. It "exploits" innovation. Here's the definition (Kenton, 2020) that suits our purposes:

> *"Commercialization is the process of bringing new products or services to market. The broader act of commercialization entails production, distribution, marketing, sales, customer support, and other key functions critical to achieving the commercial success of the new product or service."*

Your focus is on the exploitation of innovation for commercial purposes. Ideally, these commercial purposes are achieved through the creation, launch and growth of a minimal new product or service. Don't be seduced by the vapours in your "labs": *the smell's only useful if it intoxicates some commercial teams.*

THE INNOVATION → COMMERCIALISATION PROCESS

What happens when someone says, *"I have an idea!"* There's a process; there's always a process.

The business case to launch an innovation project ideally bound for commercialisation should be simple. I've mentioned business cases a few times before. But now it's time to semi-formalise the process.

But before we start, take a look at the *business case template* your company uses to vet ideas, projects, products and services. How long is it? If it's long – like more than five pages long – you don't really want to commercialise innovations. Short business cases are green lights; long ones are red. Did you hear that? Sometimes the need for process constrains our innovation and commercialisation work. When that's the case, you need to seek and destroy elaborate business cases and replace them with cases that accelerate the innovation and commercialisation processes.

Here are five questions for your *ideation business case*:

1. What's the problem?
2. What's the business approach – a new process, a new business model?
3. What's the technical approach – which technologies will be leveraged?
4. What's the financial and competitive impact?
5. What are the do/don't-do risks?

These questions apply to each stage of the commercialisation process where the business case morphs to a business plan (see Figure 18).

The exploitation of innovation for commercial purposes is where this playbook lives, as suggested in Figure 19. It's a simple view of the relationship between innovation and entrepreneurialism and the major focus here.

THE PITCH

Pitching a business case for a new idea is challenging to put it mildly, and – while I hate to begin with an emphasis on *form* versus an implied disinterest in *content* or, said differently, *style* over *substance* – but form

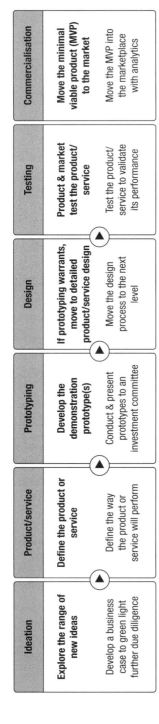

Figure 18 Innovation → commercialisation

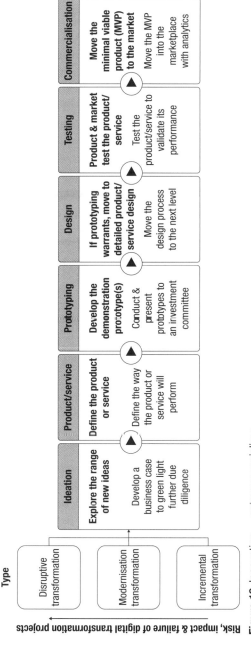

Figure 19 Innovation → entrepreneurialism

and style are hugely important, especially to investment teams who are generally more impressed with a sweet appetiser than a real meal. Snarky comments aside, it's obviously important to *"pitch"* really well.

Here are the basics:

- Understand the form and content that the audience expects. Ask those who have previously presented to your audience and solicit their ideas about what works and what doesn't. *Ask the audience directly what they want to hear and how they'd like to hear it (which means you must be able to immediately adapt to requests).* Ask how much time your audience has. Ask about the *"must knows"* and always ask about what infuriates them most about innovation pitches. (Actually, you should already know what infuriates them.)

- *Prepare for the unexpected.* Be flexible. Make sure that whoever is doing the presentation is smart, articulate and confident – but never arrogant. *If the presenter is a linear-organised presenter, find another one capable of responding to non-linear, unexpected insights, questions and events.*

- *Demonstration prototypes – "demos" – are essential to communicating innovation and selling investors on the uniqueness of entrepreneurial endeavours.* Everyone needs to "see" the plan to design, develop and sell. *They need to see how the technology solves problems in a problem-solving context.*

- One of the best ways to assess new business models, processes and technologies is to assess their potential in context, that is, how they could solve classes of problems across multiple vertical industries and even disrupt whole industry business models and processes.

- *Scenarios, simulations and use cases communicate potential.* For example, business technologists should explain how an app might help an insurance company reach more customers, how a security tool works for a company's supply chain, or how social media listening technology can enhance data analytics.

- You should also develop *live, flexible demonstrations* that clearly indicate how your new company's products and services can be changed and improved. *Flexible demos are convincing. Canned demos beg way too many questions – and undermine trust.*

- *Demos should be "board grade", that is, understandable by boards of directors and other executives who comprehend business models/processes and technologies at a high level.* Said differently, business models/processes and technologies must be demystified. Jargon and acronyms should be minimised. Examples should be straightforward and very easy to understand.

- *Failing-fast-and-cheap is a favourite investment strategy. Investment committees love the idea of investing very little time and money to learn a lot in a short period of time.* Due diligence is a process that prospective clients and investors understand and implement whenever a simulation and demo graduate to pilot status. *Anticipate audience drift toward due diligence questions – a good sign – and pre-empt drift with solid answers.*

- The pitch itself must be *"active". It cannot consist of 25 dead PowerPoint slides with tons of text and graphics on every slide. By this time, everyone expects pitches to be brief and to the point – aligned ideally to the audience's investment strategy catechism.* It should have links to graphics and videos with embedded use case-based demonstrations. A client's testimonial is also effective. (Try Prezi as an alternative to PowerPoint, but be careful that the tool doesn't confuse the message.)

- *Make sure you always dry run your pitch. Find some outsiders to inspect the words and music of your pitch play. Listen to their reviews. Adjust, as always, recognising there's no such thing as a perfect pitch.*

At the end of the day, everyone – usually some kind of investment committee – wants to know the following.
Typical investment committee questions:

- *How much money can we make?*
    - What's the likely ROI?
    - What are the best case/worst case scenarios? Quantify the win/lose scenarios, noting that a 25 per cent ROI will not sell.

- *What's the size of the market?*
    - What's the target problem?
    - How big and profitable is the target market?
    - How many competitors are in the market now?
    - How fast are new competitors entering – and leaving – the market?

- How fast are their revenues growing? Or shrinking?
- Are there any initial clients/customers we can speak with?

- *What's the new, big idea?*
  - New technology?
  - New services?
  - Hybrid delivery model?
  - Is there any IP? If so, what's the status of the IP?
  - What's the irresistible value proposition?

- *How much money – and for what?*
  - How much money is required to launch?
  - What's the expected monthly cash burn over the next 12 months?
  - What's your expected burn rate, revenue and profitability over the next five years?
  - How do you plan to spend the money? Why?
  - What's the overall fundraising plan?

- *How experienced and successful is the team?*
  - Who's on the ideation team, the delivery team, the board of directors and the advisory board? What is their combined entrepreneurial history?
  - Who are the references very familiar with the founding team's experiences whom we can contact?
  - Wrap your answers in a brisk, flexible, fun, visual pitch – and then go with the unpredictable flow.

INNOVATION LESSONS FROM DARPA

I spent some time at *DARPA* (the Defense Advanced Research Projects Agency) early in my career (Wikipedia, 2022). Everyone likes to talk about *DARPA's* approach to innovation (Dugan and Gabriel, 2013). *DARPA* brought us the internet, drones, global positioning, and a bunch of other very cool stuff that arguably enabled the entire digital revolution. For many of us, *DARPA* defines innovation excellence.

But are *DARPA's* processes easily replicable?

No – but they're aspirational as hell.

The innovation lessons I took away from *DARPA* are nearly impossible for private and especially public corporations to implement: just too many things have to be true for corporate innovation to work – and they seldom are. Before we begin, let's exclude companies like *Apple*, *Google* and *Samsung* where innovation is a well-funded core competency. Aspects of their innovation processes and culture *are DARPA-like*. But when most companies try to innovate, they fail miserably and almost always tend to eventually be disrupted by start-ups, like *Amazon* or *Uber* (which themselves eventually face innovation challenges).

Let's start with motivation. As you hear the *DARPA* motivation story, think about how your innovators are motivated and rewarded for their work.

DARPA program managers are motivated by *before-and-after*-fame and *after-cool*-fortune. Really smart people are given big budgets to do amazing things. They perform because (1) they're taxpayer funded; (2) there's a world-class *DARPA* ecosystem (*DARPA*, its *DOD* test clients, and its industry and university partners) that rewards cool stuff; and (3) once the ecosystem nods approval, *DARPA* professionals get to monetise their success with university positions, university grants, high-paying industry positions and, if they choose, other government positions with greater budgets and power. It's a well-understood motivational model – with minimal risk to the innovators or the sponsors. If their ideas actually turn out to be cool, there's a lot of personal fame in the process too. Many *DARPA* program managers love technological fame, and there's no shortage of fame to go around.

Implied in the *DARPA* innovation model is the acceptability of failure because, let's be honest, it's taxpayers' money and because no one gets it right every time. Failing is OK, not just because it's part of the culture, but because failure is a non-zero-sum game: my blowing a few million on a failed project doesn't take a nickel out of my – or my boss's – pocket. If you lose $25 million, the same thing is true – but not in industry: everyone notices a $25,000,000 write-off – and, if you do it a few times, *you're* written off (unless you're someone's best friend).

Motivating beyond the obvious – compensation and stock – is tough for most companies to understand. It's also tough for companies to actually "approve" failure, even though they usually state "for the record" that they're willing to risk millions on innovative efforts – even if they fail. Corporate innovators are financially and politically constrained from the moment they get the innovation assignment.

Motivation and money are intertwined. Money creates freedom. At *DARPA*, while we had to pitch ideas to office directors and the director of the agency, everyone assumed there was always money to pursue what a very small number of people believed were good ideas. The nonsense we hear all the time that funding follows good ideas is ridiculous: the best innovation cultures assume the opposite, that there's a pile of cash just waiting to be spent, that *will* be spent on something, that there's no grovelling for "demo" project funding that may or may not lead to "Phase 2". No SWOT charting, please. Such tools are designed to reduce risk, not innovate: if your company passes ideas through SWOT filters, it's not innovating. Put another way, innovation is not reactive, staged or managed. It's proactive and unwieldy with poorly defined and ideally unanticipated, though impactful, outcomes – if you're lucky. Yes, *lucky*. Never discount the role that luck plays in the innovation process. But *luck* is an expensive attribute of innovation.

Most companies have a really tough time pre-funding ill-defined innovation. Most companies want to "manage" innovation the way they manage the construction of a new factory. It never works. Most companies despise the idea of investing in "luck".

At *DARPA*, really smart people rotate in and out of the agency. Typically, they're already part of the *DARPA* ecosystem. They've generally proven their value from high-profile scientific, engineering or technology projects – their passport into the ecosystem. If you turn out to be *relatively* unintelligent at *DARPA*, you're marginalised. You can fail, but you must be smart. Many companies, on the other hand, frequently reward style over substance, relationships over performance.

Sometimes, the innovation "assignment" is even given to long-standing corporate cronies. The idea of taking the best and brightest salespersons, supply-chain managers or customer service experts and giving them a *DARPA*-like two-to-three-year assignment to just think about new ways to do old things worries stock chaperones to no end. The in-house corporate "innovation team" is often mediocre and therefore destined to fail. (Now's the time to take a hard look at your "innovators".)

Most companies find it difficult, if not impossible, to grant "sabbaticals" to groups of "hi-pos" (high potentials) – or even lo-pos, for that matter. They want to keep them on the line generating profits when it's precisely the best and the brightest who should own innovation.

DARPA loves small teams, sometimes comprise a single scientist, engineer or technologist (with some supporting members from the ecosystem). Big companies love big teams with explicit governance about who gets to say and do what/when/where. Many *DARPA* professionals are, I dare say, intellectually arrogant. In fact, they're paid to misbehave. I can still remember discussions where geniuses crushed highly intelligent people. Most companies don't like this kind of dialogue – at least face-to-face: most corporate battles are fought behind the scenes where clever people leverage their tenure, their relationships and their personal styles to get what they want. *DARPA* is much more of an intellectual meritocracy than most companies, regardless of how companies perceive themselves. In fact, the assumption at *DARPA* is that individuals can often carry the innovation load all by themselves, though obviously the *DARPA* ecosystem is continuously leveraged.

Most companies would never trust a huge innovation budget to one person, regardless of how smart, glib or connected they were. Most companies would never allow innovation efforts to just "float" out there over long periods of time with no "governance". Companies need to control budgets, people and processes – which is why they usually fail so spectacularly at innovation.

At *DARPA*, innovation is not a set of activities, it's an attitude, a culture, supported by a set of loose processes and even less-defined outcomes. Most corporate cultures are, therefore, by definition, anything but innovative. In fact, corporate cultures are designed to be repeatable, consistent, predictable and profitable. They're also designed to be scalable, but only within limits.

Self-disruption is not a competency many companies have, which is why most innovation is de facto or de jure outsourced to those with separate vested financial interests. It's also nearly impossible for "successful" companies to cannibalise their revenue streams, even if there's consensus that the streams are not permanent. Print media, for example, still doubles down on print-driven business models, while just about everyone knows that the death of print media correlates perfectly with the rising death rate of today's consumers of print media.

The argument here is simple. Successful companies become successful because they optimise routines in relatively stable markets, not because they continuously search for new ways to replace old, profitable processes or when they should eliminate profitable SKUs because "it's time". The corporate financial structure is biased against innovation. They're convinced that they can "re-engineer", "reinvent" and "innovate" at will when nothing could be further from the truth. They almost always need a lot of outside help to change processes, products and services and, even when there's help, they usually fail.

While very few companies will ever become *DARPA*-like, there are valuable lessons we can learn from perhaps the greatest innovation machine in the history of technology.

Aspirational for sure.

TECHNOLOGY TEAMS IN ACTION

Two truths prevail: innovation is the lifeblood of growth, and stagnation is a clear and present danger to profitable growth. No company can escape these truths: they must innovate if they expect to grow their revenue. Examples of companies that fell from grace because they failed to innovate and commercialise (Valuer.ai, 2022), include *Kodak, Xerox, Nokia, Blockbuster, Yahoo, Segway, JC Penny, IBM, Tie Rack, Blackberry, MySpace, Commodore, Sears, Macy's, Hitachi, Polaroid, Toshiba, RadioShack, Motorola, Borders, Palm, Sony, National Geographic, Pan Am, Circuit City, Netscape, Toys R Us, AOL* and *Atari*, among so many others. The innovation imperative is real.

Smart companies – hopefully yours – have dedicated emerging technology teams that track and pilot technologies.

Ideally, these teams pursue the following activities:

- **Track technology.** Technology trackers are responsible for identifying, tracking and assessing existing and emerging digital technologies. ET teams perform constant, automated web searches, attend technology conferences and speak with technology experts across the globe. Technology trackers are partially "embedded" in the lines of business they serve.

- **Develop technology trends maps.** Trackers are responsible for scanning their industry with a specific focus on direct, indirect and emerging competitors. The tracking team is responsible for identifying the most promising digital technologies. Figure 20 presents a notional technology investment playbook. Note how the guide categorises technologies according to their maturity and the business impact they might have. These two broad metrics are used to guide ET teams about tracking, assessment (for tracking) and piloting. Note that the list of technologies changes over time. Some will be added and some will fall off the list. The key metric is the movement of technologies across the guide from tracking to assessment to piloting. Once a technology reaches maturity and

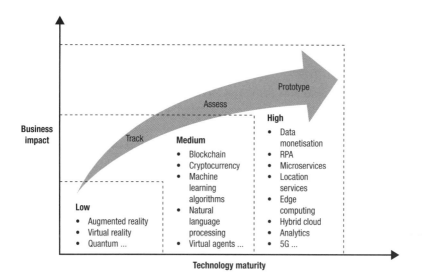

Figure 20 Notional technology investment guide

once it can be linked with a high-impact business problem, it's handed off to the ET team members who pilot technologies.

■ **Prototype technology.** Emerging technology team members work closely with the technology tracking team to prioritise demonstrations of the most promising technologies. The team coordinates with the lines of business (LOBs) about which prototypes might yield the most impactful business results. The technology prototyping team conducts demonstrations designed to determine the readiness of the technologies for full deployment. The team develops business cases for proposed technology pilots. The team conducts pilots that will – if successful – become nominees for full deployment. Prototypes transition technology that enables innovation – the major goal of the ET team.

■ **Development of the company's architecture.** This is the focus of the enterprise architecture team and comprises business processes, data, applications and the delivery of its products and services. The enterprise architecture team "governs" innovation investments. Enterprise architecture is jointly developed by the ET team, the Office of Strategy and the department of Information Technology (IT). The enterprise architecture team works closely with the Strategy and IT teams to produce the business, data, applications and delivery architectures. The enterprise architecture is a framework for organising and optimising technology investments. While EA is traditionally internally focused designed to align business and technology, EA is internally *and* externally focused especially on innovative products and services.

■ **Explanation and communication of all ET activities.** This is the focus of the technology relationship management team and includes the development of technology hype-cycles, its technology pilots and the enterprise architecture. Technology relationship managers document and translate activities, requirements, capabilities and the progress of the ET team for consumption by the rest of the company. They are the ET newscasters and ambassadors. Technology relationship managers within the ET team are outward facing, with direct and continuous coordination responsibilities with the Office of Strategy, the Office of Innovation, IT and other parts of their company.

Innovation and commercialisation depend upon emerging technology. Emerging technology teams are the instruments of innovation and therefore digital transformation. ET teams should be composed of professionals with a variety of skills and competencies. The teams must also find homes. As Christensen suggests:

> *"Place the disruptive technology into an autonomous organization . . . allow the disruption organization to utilize all of the company's resources when needed."*

ET teams should function relatively independently from other corporate organisations. They should be led by a Chief Technology Officer whose role is to manage innovation under the direction of a chief innovation officer or the chief executive officer (CEO). ET teams also need funding for which there are alternative models. Funding can come as an equal tax to the lines of business or funded directly by the office of innovation. It can also come directly from the CEO. Innovation is frequently pursued at the direction of the board of directors.

Regardless of their homes or sources of funding, ET teams must earn credibility, and the best way to do this is to track, pilot and deploy technology that impacts business models and processes in ways that save money or make money for the lines of business. Once a track record is established, ET teams will rise in stature and importance – which are the ultimate enabling innovation/commercialisation metrics.

GOVERNANCE

Governance is a key performance measure of every ET team, which is accountable for technology tracking, process/technology matching and piloting. ET teams are also responsible for deployment. The distinction between accountability and responsibility is important because it implies ownership. In addition to these two governance categories are "consulted" and "informed", which round out the popular RACI chart categories (Hayworth, 2018) which consists of designations of who is "**r**esponsible", "**a**ccountable", "**c**onsulted" and "**i**nformed" for projects and programs. The RACI chart in Figure 21 describes the relationships that the ET team has with its internal partners.

The ET team works closely with the office of innovation (often run by a Chief Innovation Officer), the office of strategy and especially the chief information officer who typically runs the entire IT (information technology) organisation. Emerging technology must be unambiguously governed by these stakeholders. The RACI chart describes the relationships among the stakeholders clearly. Note that the ET team is accountable for the overall ET strategy, technology tracking, technology piloting and the design of the enterprise architecture – and responsible for the deployment of successful technology pilots.

Stakeholders Tasks	Emerging technology team	Office of innovation	Office of strategy	Information technology team
FT strategy	A	R	C	R
Technology tracking	A	R	C	R
Technology piloting	A	R	C	R
Enterprise architecture	A	R	C	R
Deployment	R	R	C	A

Responsible ☐ Accountable ☑ Consulted ☒ Informed

Figure 21 RACI chart for ET governance

INNOVATION/COMMERCIALISATION PLAYS

Innovation is not commercialisation; innovation enables commercialisation – not the other way around.

There are three distinct kinds of innovation: incremental innovation, innovation that results from modernisation and disruptive innovation.

Commercialisation is different. It represents the pivot from innovation. It "exploits" innovation: "Commercialisation is the process of bringing new products or services to market."

Focus on the exploitation of innovation for commercial purposes. Ideally, these commercial purposes are achieved through the creation, launch and growth of a minimal viable product (MVP) or service.

The business case to launch an innovation project ideally bound for commercialisation should be simple.

Pitching a business case for a new idea is challenging: understand the form and content that the audience expects. Prepare for the unexpected. Demonstration prototypes – "demos" – are essential to communicating innovation and selling investors on the uniqueness of entrepreneurial endeavours. Everyone needs to "see" the plan to design, develop and sell. They need to see how the technology solves problems in a problem-solving context. Demos should be "board grade", that is, understandable by boards of directors and other executives who comprehend business models/processes and technologies at a high level. Smart companies have dedicated emerging technology (ET) teams that track and pilot technologies.

Governance is a key performance measure of every ET team, which is accountable for technology tracking, piloting, the enterprise architecture and pilots.

RACI charts can be helpful with the governance of innovation and commercialisation.

CHAPTER 9

FIND, RETAIN AND REWARD THE TALENT YOU NEED

CHAPTER SUMMARY

- *There are talent gaps between what you need and what you have.*
- *There are five talent areas of huge importance to your success: (1) business strategy, models and processes; (2) disruptive technologies; (3) pilots; (4) cloud delivery; and (5) strategic management.*
- *AI/machine learning and the algorithms that enable it are uniquely important.*
- *Recruit talent in four additional areas: (1) privacy and surveillance; (2) misinformation/disinformation; (3) diversity, inclusion and equality; and (4) people management.*
- *Recruit, retain and reward the best talent across a broad spectrum of activities.*

GAPS

Once upon a time, a general partner of a private equity venture capital fund *(focused on investing in internet companies)* called me into his office and whispered, "*Steve, what's the internet . . . what does it do . . . how does it work?*" Another partner at the same firm smugly declared that, "*No one likes shopping online . . . people will always want to go to stores.*" Fortunately, these "Bizarro World" experiences occurred some years ago. But what about today? If you asked PEVC partners to explain multi-cloud management, could they do it? What about automated supply chains and their impact on scalability? Or how machine learning enables robotic process automation? One of the dirty little secrets of the PEVC world is how little partners actually know about technology. The same is true of C-suiters *and* even those in the technology trenches – *your* trenches. The depth of technology knowledge is quite shallow, even within companies who depend upon technology for their livelihoods. I could tell a hundred stories about how little those in charge of technology spending actually knew about technology. I could tell stories right now about how it's gotten worse.

Companies that worry about business-technology gaps sometimes perform "work force analyses". They do this when they believe there's a growing gap between the technology they need and the skills and competencies of their technology teams. What do they find? What would *you* find?

If we performed a workforce analysis across the twentieth and twenty-first centuries, what would we discover? The lists below identify the talent you once required versus the talent you need today. (It also sets the stage for the assessment you should conduct right now.)

In the twentieth century you:

- Built, deployed, maintained and upgraded software applications.

- Defined, architected and supported our own computing and communications infrastructures.

- Owned and ran your own data centres with backup generators.

- Supported descriptive database management systems; you seldom focused on predictive analytics.

- Rarely thought about real-time transaction processing.

- Obsessed about software development methodologies.

- Invented tools, platforms and "workbenches" to accelerate software development.

- Mocked and feared open-source software.

- Did not imagine social media.

- Automated virtually nothing.

- Insisted upon defining detailed "user" requirements and then documenting them (over and over again) in complicated almost archaic symbols and notations.

- Believed that user requirements were fixed and once we "discovered" them, all we had to do was satisfy them in software.

- Insisted upon "governance" where roles and responsibilities around technology acquisition, deployment and support were tightly defined: you liked software standards.

- Were willing to let vendors define our business processes and overall business models in really big software applications, like enterprise resource planning (ERP) and customer relationship management (CRM) applications.

- Expected technology stability and consistency – once you got operational "IT" right.

But in the twenty-first century, everything changed. You now:

- Rent applications.

- Seldom directly maintain or upgrade applications.

- Yield your infrastructures to cloud and communications network providers.

- Close your data centres and sell your generators.

- Obsess with explanatory, predictive and prescriptive analytics.

- Pay dearly for real-time transaction processing.

- Track all things social.

- Manage software developers: you no longer do software development.

- Give your software development tools, platforms and "work benches" to your platform-as-a-service (PaaS) providers.

- Cede requirements to packaged vendors who've moved their applications to the cloud.

- Continuously track – and pilot – emerging and potentially disruptive technologies.

- Want business agility and flexibility – and the technology that enables both.

- Accept "small" (micro-services) software as you cut the cords to "big" (monolithic) software.

- Outsource way too much to consultants.

- Fully accept, and commit to, open-source appliances and applications (and love *Apache* and *Google*).

- See no distinction between business and technology and technology and business.

- Distribute technology governance internally and externally: seldom standardise software.

The talent differences between the twentieth and twenty-first centuries are striking – and growing: to which century – honestly – is your team best suited?

Take a hard look at your team. How many of them understand cloud service level agreements (SLAs), container technology and cloud performance metrics? How much experience does the team have negotiating with alternative cloud providers? How deeply does the team understand alternative cloud architectures? Does the team have the skills and competencies to communicate with business managers and executives? Does the team fully comprehend cloud and other security risks? How many data scientists do you have on staff? Do you understand the reach (and risk) of social media? How committed are you to real-time transaction processing? Intelligent algorithms? (What are *they*?) What's the emerging/disruptive technology piloting strategy? The answer to these and related questions is "no" – and you know it. (And before you forget, what's the state of your business-technology strategy and the business models and processes derived from the strategy? How many strategists, modellers and process miners/managers do you have?)

At the end of the day, you must identify and plug the gaps as soon as you discover them. You must answer five simple questions:

1. Do I have the right people?
2. How many of the wrong ones do I have?
3. How do I plug the gaps as quickly as possible?
4. How do I keep them?
5. How do I reward them?

A poor, or dishonest, talent assessment process is a game-breaker. If you're unwilling to make hard decisions about who's on the field, you will lose every game you play. If you're unwilling to invest in talent, you should stop playing altogether.

FIVE ESSENTIAL TALENTS

Business technologists should talk about technology only in the context of business strategy, models and processes. Twentieth-century technologists spoke about operational technology as painkillers that had to be tightly managed. These were unhappy discussions that everyone dreaded, and often ended with complaints about the cost of technology *and not what technology could do for the business.*

Digital technology is a business solution, not a problem, and should be presented that way. Digital technologies that fall into the painkiller-versus-vitamin-pill trap will quickly discover just how sceptical some (especially "older") executives can be about the cost-versus-benefit of digital technology – even today. Business technologists should also appreciate the importance of bottom lines.

Business managers and executives need to understand how digital technology will help or hurt the business not just in terms of costs versus business benefits, but also in terms of risks. (Note that managers and executives are now keenly interested in digital security because breaches threaten their companies and their careers.) Speaking digital requires a new interpretation of traditional SWOT analyses. Executives also crave information about disruptive technologies, especially the ones their arch rivals are deploying. Digital technologists should be corporate spies.

They should be business internal consultants with deep industry domain expertise. They should displace the external consultants that sit on your long talent benches only too willing to jump into the game – for a fee, of course. (Yes, this is another example of brains versus brawn.)

Perhaps very surprisingly, and unlike operational "IT", strategic technology requires less precision. Since we've moved to cloud delivery, we no longer need to know who made the servers that host our applications or how often they need to be replaced. Such details are meaningless today. Twentieth-century operational technologists were obsessed with server vendors, maintenance, backup and recovery; no one cares about such things when the business goal is competitive performance: your hired brawn is now responsible for all hardware and software delivery issues.

Fortunately, this means that deploying a new application no longer requires long discussions about software development methodologies or whether the offshore programmers can handle requirements. Debates about cloud security are appropriate and necessary, but should be more about industry *compliance* than security *technology*. Cloud delivery has forever changed the nature and level of technology conversations since the cloud itself provides all the technology plumbing necessary to enable and optimise business processes. While we agonised in the twentieth century about plumbing, today we can focus on architects and strategists without the distraction of leaky pipes.

Digital technologists should focus on new technology, new technology delivery platforms, and the strategic role that technology can play toward competitiveness and profitability. While the list will change over time, there's a set of technology opportunities that should be on every digital technologist's list. Think of them as talking points, objectives *and* talent requirements.

There are five:

1. Business strategy, models and processes.
2. Existing and disruptive technologies.
3. Demonstration pilots through prototyping.
4. Cloud delivery.
5. Strategic management.

These five areas describe your business technology world and the talent you need to win. Let's describe them:

1. Business strategy, models and processes

   You need people who understand your business domain, the strategies of "as is" and "to be" competitors in your industry and current and future business models and processes; such people must also understand the methods, tools and software platforms that enable the description of "as is" and invention "to be" business strategies, models and processes – and technologies.

2. Existing and disruptive technologies

   Talent here assumes an awareness and basic understanding of current and emerging digital technologies as well as how to "match" technologies to "as is" and "to be" processes. This is collaborative talent that works closely with your strategists, modellers and process miners/managers.

3. Demonstration pilots through prototyping

   This talent requires your team to design and implement Stage 1 (demonstration) prototypes with tools that enable the presentation of "demos". It also requires the team to understand (short) business cases and stage-gates as a way to measure progress along the continuum toward minimum viable products (MVPs). This talent appreciates innovation but commercialisation more.

4. Cloud delivery

   This talent requires teams to understand all things cloud, including especially the cloud's ability to deliver emerging technologies suitable for prototyping.

5. Strategic management

   Talent here requires a wide and deep understanding of brains versus brawn, and the ability to create and manage the overall business-technology delivery strategy.

These five areas are the ones you send to your recruiters for talent acquisition. They're also the filter through which you conduct talent assessments.

While it's tempting to assign equal weights to the five areas described above, in reality, the areas can – and should – be rank-ordered. The first and second areas – (1) business strategy, models and processes and (2) existing and disruptive technologies – are rank-ordered higher than the rest for two reasons: there's a relatively poor understanding of the relationship among competitiveness, profitability, strategy, models and processes, and technology; and because there's a shortage of talent in these areas. Said a little differently: you need them, and they're hard to find.

SPECIAL TALENT

There are always some areas that require special attention. Today – and for the foreseeable future – one of those areas is AI and machine learning, including the algorithms that make them smart. Why these two? Because AI and machine learning is a game-changer and because algorithms power some of the most important plays of the game.

AI will fundamentally change transaction processing through the automation of many routine tasks individuals and companies perform all the time. It's also poised to graduate to much more complex tasks.

It's important your team understand the potential of AI/ML, but there's likely a gap in your team's understanding of the relationship between digital business models – which are pervasive – and the quasi- and fully-automated algorithmic-based solutions available to you.

Figure 22 describes the capabilities of AI/ML and the most popular algorithms used to solve a variety of problems. It's likely that very few members of your team understand the range of algorithms in Figure 22 or how they work, which means they cannot match the right algorithm to the right business process that needs to be improved, modified, automated or replaced. Nor can your team easily discuss the strengths and weaknesses of classes of algorithms or specific algorithms which are mysterious to most of the technology professionals even today. The stakes are high: success depends almost completely upon successful business model/ business algorithm matching – upon a marriage between models and algorithms.

Find AI/ML/algorithm talent that can take three steps:

1. Identify and explain existing and emerging digital business models and how they work.

   There are classes of business models that industries are adopting. They have characteristics that executives should understand – even as their companies deploy them. Step 1 will identify and describe the models, including their trajectories.

2. Identify and explain the range of business algorithms that enable digital business models and processes.

   There are algorithms embedded in applications and platforms that enable, improve, automate and replace business processes and whole business models. Note that we cannot expect executives to fully understand all of the algorithms in Figure 22, or the underlying

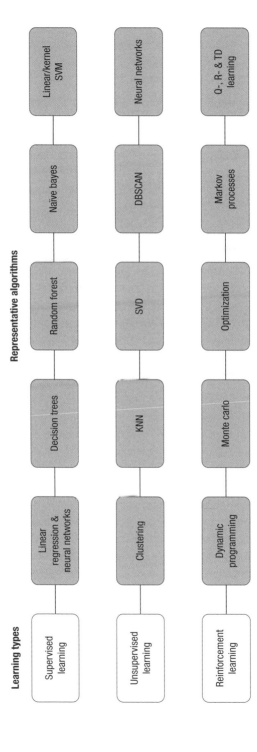

Figure 22 AI and machine learning algorithms

mathematics that powers them. But we can expect them to understand classes of algorithms and generally how they work (defined by the data they require, the way data are processed and analysed, and the kind of results they generate).

Note the number of algorithms and whole classes of algorithms in Figure 22. Your team should understand what the classes do, how they work, the problems to which they're best suited and the results they produce. The team does not need to understand the computational components of the hundreds of algorithms that populate the computer, data and machine learning sciences.

3. Identify and explain the relationships across digital business models and algorithmic solutions.

   This is the key step. Building on Steps 1 and 2, this step will present problem scenarios to your team (comprising expected outcomes, data, processing, etc.) and "exercise" the selection of algorithms. The process will not expect the team to perform perfect matches, but will require them to think about the strengths and weaknesses of algorithmic classes and the (business model) problem characteristics that best work together.

As new methods, tools and techniques make their way onto the business stage, as business processes become increasingly automated and as competitive advantage is defined around algorithmic competency, you need to know how this important business problem-solving toolbox works, and which tools are the most powerful and best suited to their business models and processes. It's essential that you understand the potential of machine learning/automation along with all related solutions. It's a new world with new business models, new business processes and whole new algorithmic solutions that optimise business models and processes. The trick is to know which ones to use to solve specific problems. As machine learning and automation explode, you need to understand as much as you can about digital business models and the business algorithms that enable, improve and replace them.

You must find, retain and reward talent that understands as much as possible about digital business models and the business algorithms that enable, improve and replace them.

DON'T FORGET PRIVACY, MISINFORMATION, DIVERSITY AND PEOPLE MANAGEMENT TALENT

Here's some additional talent you should find, retain and reward:

- Privacy and surveillance talent.
- Misinformation/disinformation talent.
- Diversity, inclusion and equality talent.
- People management talent.

PRIVACY AND SURVEILLANCE TALENT

While the USA needs to pass the equivalent of the general data privacy regulation (GDPR), you also need to think carefully about the tension between your business models and the monetisation of customer data. This will likely lead nowhere for companies (perhaps yours) who make their money from the data they collect from customers and monetise in a variety of ways, but many companies can still rethink their commitment to privacy.

You also need to address the growing surveillance culture. Are you collecting information about your employees, vendors, suppliers and customers in ways that should worry them – and you? While data privacy is about data monetisation, surveillance is about the collection of data. Where are the cameras, the digital eavesdroppers and systems monitors? Should you, for example, deploy facial recognition technology? These are complex questions that should not be passed through just a single filter called "profitability". You need talent that understands these issues.

MISINFORMATION/DISINFORMATION TALENT

The need for regulation in the area of misinformation is screaming from every broadcast tower in the world. The problem, of course – again concerns business models that depend upon misinformation (or worse), such as media that win by attracting as many participants as possible. You should be aware that your words, policies and actions may contribute to misinformation and disinformation. You should be extremely careful about the "sides" you choose. You should be acutely aware that the words and actions have consequences. While this should seem obvious, you should never engage in behaviour that threatens your revenue streams, brand and, ultimately, your profitability.

DIVERSITY, INCLUSION AND EQUALITY TALENT

Awareness here is crucial to success in several ways. Frist, there is the power of diversity, inclusion and equality (DEI) simply because it enables perspective and creativity – commodities always in short supply. DEI is also a good business practice for internal harmony and external brand management. Worse, ignoring DEI can have serious consequences that you must respect. Said differently, DEI provides opportunities for you to compete.

PEOPLE MANAGEMENT TALENT

There is no more important foundational step you can take to improve the positioning of your company than recruiting and retaining the most talented professionals in their industry. But are you even aware of their talent requirements and gaps? Have you developed talent requirements matrices to measure your capabilities and gaps going forward? Are you objective about your teams? Research suggests that companies have an extremely difficult time assessing their people objectively or consistently. You should serve as an example here and stop rewarding friends over high performers – which the research describes as an unfortunate, repeatable practice across industries. Ongoing investments in talent are also essential, especially those designed to keep the talent pool fresh and incentivised. If you fail to replenish and revitalise talent you will lose market share. Awareness here is as important as it's ever been. You need help managing all this.

FIND THE RIGHT TALENT

The continuous search for talent is now a core competency. You must search for talent every day. Years ago, operational technology talent was more plentiful than strategic technology talent is today. The challenge is to find the right talent, keep the talent and reward talent in ways that keep them focused on the strategic mission. But there's a shortage – as *McKinsey* (2022) warns you:

"Business leaders are feeling the heat. According to a McKinsey survey of more than 1,500 senior executives globally, some 87 percent say their companies are not adequately prepared to address the skill gap.

"Despite the formidable challenges in finding tech talent, incumbent companies cannot expect to succeed in the digital world without being technologically strong, which is simply not possible without a deep bench of tech talent. In fact, developing robust people and talent strategies are among the highest-value actions a business can take."

Finding talent has become a sales and marketing activity. It's talent focused, which means, among other things, that you have to accommodate candidates far more than ever before. As virtual and remote communications become standard, candidates may want to stay where they are instead of moving to a new city. As described in *Fortune Magazine* (2021):

"Not everyone really wants to be living in one of these big cities or can even afford in the beginning to break into it . . . remote work has opened up a lot of options for employers to just find the best talent and also to open it up to a more diverse set of candidates."

There are also opportunities to upskill existing talent, though this option must be carefully assessed:

"If a company can't recruit enough people with the tech skills they need, why not look within the company to find people who can be taught these critical skills? . . . internal candidates for upskilling into tech roles also offer the immense benefit of already knowing the operations of the company. This makes these employees strong candidates for leadership down the road."

Whole new methods are now in play:

"Operationally, companies with sophisticated talent strategies are now focused on candidate experience and emphasizing quality-of-hire metrics over speed-of-hire."

Beyond talent accommodations, there are other steps you can take to find the talent you need, such as developing relationships with colleges and universities that produce students with the right educational backgrounds to satisfy your requirements. *Tesla* is an excellent example of business-university partnerships. Like many companies, *Tesla's* recruiting strategy begins with internships and early employment offers. They also like Co-op programs where students experience work as part of their undergraduate education. Engineering, technology and finance majors are always in demand while "management" majors are increasingly difficult to differentiate.

"Tesla (Quora, 2022) generally like the following . . .

"They want you to come on board after your internship (as long as you performed average or better). The time and effort to train an intern is really expensive, and the company is always hiring.

"They like colleges with programs that integrate industry experience into the undergraduate/graduate curriculum. For example, many Canadian universities require students to complete CoOps before they graduate. The ideal situation for Tesla would be if you did that required coop after

all your coursework, but before you graduate. So that once you complete the internship and performed well, they can immediately extend an offer.

"They generally like juniors, seniors, master's, PhD's for their interns. You know enough to know what's going on, plus you'll be looking for full time soon.

"(For the sake of this point, I will choose MechEng.) Every school will have a different mechanical engineering program. For example, I know that Boston University graduates students and many go off to industry. Their curriculum has manufacturing/supply chain courses. On the other hand, my school at UC San Diego is heavy research-based institution. We do not have a manufacturing/supply chain course. No MechEng undergrad graduates with an exposure to what manufacturing is. Tesla does not visit UCSD as often. However, I still got an internship, and I'm a biomedical engineer."

Can you "customise" the form and content of the students you might like to hire? Can you influence the content of curriculum? You can provide the above-referenced internships and co-ops, and you can join advisory boards and similar organisations. You can endow professorships, name classrooms, buildings and whole colleges. Pipelines are for sale. Relationships can be developed and nurtured over time. My university's School of Business places a staggering number of students at *PwC*, *KPMG*, *EY* and *Deloitte* – year after year. Internships are a way of life at these companies – and our students. We also place students at investment banks and consultancies (where I hope they provide cost-effective brawn and, eventually, valuable brains). Advisory boards provide ideas and "guidance" to faculty and administrators. Faculty are sometimes hired as consultants. These relationships are beneficial to universities, faculty and students.

You must pursue as many talent channels and pipelines as possible, including relationships with search firms, former employees and the technology associations that advance the skills and competencies you need.

You should also add some criteria to your recruitment lists. While business-technology skills and competencies – the five essential areas – should dominate your search, you should also recruit professionals with solid communications skills as well as personalities that synchronise the best into your companies.

GROW THE RIGHT TALENT

As strange as it might seem, you might consider educating and training your own professionals through the establishment of a "university" of your own. Some companies have developed their own "curriculum" used to reskill and upskill technologists. If you understand business-technology trends – which you should – then you can develop "courses" that will keep employees current. Decisions about who to reskill and upskill is another hard one. Some of your team might be more than salvageable, but others are not. You know who they are. Just remember that for every unsalvageable business technologist you choose to "save", you've deprived your company of a high potential one.

RETAIN AND REWARD THE RIGHT TALENT

How to retain and reward talent is an old topic. Why? Because turnover is constant – and always disruptive and expensive.

Can you reduce turnover? Yes. But you cannot eliminate it. Accept the fact that some of your best talent will outgrow your company simply because they're the best talent. There's nothing you can do to eliminate turnover driven by ambition. You cannot offer more money, a bigger office, more responsibility or fabulous seats at rock concerts, sports events or operas (depending upon their taste). They're gone. Just wish them well and hope they return some day.

Mainstream retention is the goal. If I hear another laundry list of retention strategies and tactics, I'm going to scream. The "lists" are obvious – and largely ineffective. Some obvious suggestions include (Pratt and Florentine, 2022):

- *"Identify candidates who'll stay the course.*
- *"Identify those who share your outlook.*
- *"Provide ongoing education and clear paths to advancement.*
- *"Be competitive with compensation packages.*
- *"Deliver for your employees.*
- *"Engage your workers."*

Here are some more (Marquet, 2022):

- *"Create an engaging workplace culture that makes all team members feel welcome.*
- *"Offer competitive benefits and other attractive perks.*
- *"Provide ample opportunities for growth.*
- *"Offer employees more opportunities to use their skills.*
- *"Make sure employees have a clear understanding of their role in the company to prevent miscommunication.*
- *"Provide recognition and rewards for employees who go above and beyond their duties."*

Sound familiar?

The above suggestions have merit, but there are some others you should strongly consider.

RESPECT

The first and foremost is *respect*. The employees you want to retain must feel respected. They must be acknowledged as valuable. They must accrue the status of highly respected professionals. They must be treated differently within the organisational structure of your company. Yes, this is a performance issue that deliberately locates employees across a value continuum, that recognises "stars", "high potentials" and – dare I say – "low potentials".

SEGMENTED PERFORMANCE RECOGNITION

Closely related to respect is the second suggestion, which is to *openly value the performance of high versus low performers.* High performers resent low performers, especially when they're treated similarly to high performers, which is often regarded as a professional insult to the work high performers are proud to conduct. When obviously inferior work is rewarded in nearly the same ways as superior work, you're breeding resentment that will eventually explode into resignations.

Note that this requires you to make some hard decisions. Most corporate cultures (and the executives who inhabit them) are reluctant to publicly contrast high versus low performers. But if you want to retain the best performers, you need to make it clear to everyone just how valued they are – at the expense of those who bring little value to the game.

FLEXIBILITY

Your best and brightest business technologists should have lots of team, project and program flexibility. They should have the flexibility to choose roles as well. If they choose to avoid huge projects with enormous management responsibilities, they should be able to do so. They should have the freedom to invest in specific technologies and, perhaps, should they choose to do so, create centres of excellence. While this kind of flexibility may sound excessive, high performers crave control over their professional lives. If you want to keep them, you must yield significant control of their activities. Don't worry too much: the best business technologists are usually drawn to the most important projects.

Flexibility dovetails with respect. It's another way of recognising the special status of valuable business technologists. The ability to do what's preferred – to even chase a technology bucket-list – is an extremely important retention tool. It's also important to allow high performers to stay put where they're doing good work. This is not unlike the argument made in the Preface and elsewhere in this playbook about CIOs and CTOs who would prefer to stay in the operational trenches rather than assume whole new strategic responsibilities. The same is true of some business technologists who prefer to pursue specific work streams versus pursuing so-called "bigger" projects with more (and more) responsibility. You must be extremely careful about traditional retention methods that assume talented professionals want more (and more) responsibility. Your job is to keep talented professionals happy and productive. Understanding their preferred ways of working is key to retention, even – especially – if it means granting them the right to work the way they prefer.

REWARDS

Let's not deceive ourselves: financial rewards are the most important rewards you can bestow on your best and brightest business technologists. These rewards should be in several forms. Base salary, bonuses and stock – regardless of whether the company is public or private – should comprise the financial compensation package. Benefits should be generous as well, so generous that benefits themselves become a recruiting and retention strategy. Similar to what universities do to avoid burnout and support knowledge creation activities, you might also consider offering sabbaticals to your most valuable performers. Obviously, high performers can work from home, down the road, across the country or around the world.

Rewards should go beyond money. But here the challenge is more complicated. School-like awards should not be part of the reward package. High performers do not appreciate pieces of paper with embossed names; nor do they appreciate dedicated days of recognition or similar accolades. Such "rewards" are often actually embarrassing. Some rewards that work are project and program recognition which appear in internal newsletters and company blogs. Beyond these relatively "quiet" rewards are those your best performers might suggest. Ask them what they might like, and what they might find appropriate. Finally, make it your business to understand the personal priorities of your superstars. Major personal events in their lives should be wrapped in professional rewards. For example, if you discover that one of your stars is shopping for colleges for their children, offer long weekends for out-of-town visits to the colleges on the list.

TALENT PLAYS

Routinely perform "work force analyses" to measure the gap between the business technology expertise you need and what you have on staff.

Make sure your team has expertise in five areas:

1. Business strategy, models and processes.

2. Existing and disruptive technologies.

3. Demonstration pilots through prototyping.

4. Cloud delivery.

5. Strategic management.

You should rank-order the first and second areas – (1) business strategy, models and processes and (2) existing and disruptive technologies – higher than the other three.

AI and machine learning, including the algorithms that make them smart, should be designated special talent requirements. You also need talent in privacy and surveillance, misinformation/disinformation, diversity, inclusion and equality and people management.

You must pursue as many recruitment channels and pipelines as possible, including relationships with universities, search firms, former employees and the technology associations that advance the skills and competencies you need.

Retention should include conventional and unconventional approaches. Respect, segmented performance recognition and flexibility should be added to retention strategies. Rewards should be chiefly financial sprinkled with some rewards suggested by your superstars.

CHAPTER 10

DEVELOP
A STRATEGIC
TECHNOLOGY
GAME PLAN

CHAPTER SUMMARY

- *Failure is still pervasive.*

- *There's no more important activity than the development of a strategic technology game plan that comprises elements, processes and outcomes.*

- *Specific elements, processes and outcomes include the development of a business strategy, a business model, as-is and to-be processes, and prototyping the most promising technology/process matches.*

- *Requirements include keeping digital transformation in perspective, paying special attention to AI and machine learning, investing what you must in cybersecurity, tracking regulatory policy, leading, managing and governing the right team, innovating, and finding, retaining and rewarding the talent you need.*

- *Outcomes include improved/eliminated/automated/reinvented processes, a more competitive business model and even whole new business strategies.*

REMINDERS

Before you build your digital strategy, let's make some wake-up calls. Technology projects still fail all the time. Everyone knows this. But *why* do so many of them fail? *Why* is the learning curve so flat? Here are 10 reasons why strategic projects of all shapes and sizes fail, and why enterprise technology investments fail so spectacularly. As you read the list, ask yourself how many elephants are in the rooms where you spend all those technology dollars every year. Haven't you ever asked yourself if there's a better way?

The "elephants in the room" analogy is important. There are so many mistakes made every day, month and year that perhaps everyone's just grown immune to business as usual. Failure's been normalised. If I hear another CIO or CTO complain about their consultants, vendors and teams, I'm going to scream in real-time with a bodycam.

Let's get into it. Ask yourself how many elephants apply to you, your team and your company – and how many elephants you feed every day. In the process, ask yourself how much of the message was received loud and clear.

REMINDER #1: NO STRATEGIES, MODELS OR PROCESSES

Without a strategy, a business model and an inventory of business processes, all is lost: if you don't have – or want to develop – a strategy, a business model or an inventory of "as-is" and "to-be" processes, you should just call it quits. Without a business strategy, a business model and the identification, description and profiling of business processes that can be improved, automated, eliminated or invented with existing and emerging technology, you will fail to leverage technology investments. If you don't have this database, you're already in trouble.

REMINDER # 2: FORGOTTEN CORE COMPETENCIES

Here's the question:

"If you cannot strategise, build business models, identify and profile business processes, track technologies and identify the business-technology matches that will make you more competitive, what's your actual job?"

Consultants should not tell you how to run your business or list the technologies you should track. You should reclaim core competencies that distinguish between "brains" and "brawn", where you have the brains and consultants have the brawn. The more you outsource, the more likely you are to fail — especially if you outsource everything strategic.

REMINDER #3: OPERATIONAL TECHNOLOGY IS A COMMODITY

Operational technology is now a commodity. There's no real difference among ERP apps, BI apps and cloud providers – no matter what your vendors and consultants tell you. Stop worrying about laptops and servers and focus on strategic technology – the last differentiator.

REMINDER #4: STOP PESTERING CIOS AND CTOS TO BE "STRATEGIC"

CIOs and CTOs should stay in the operational trenches: they're not strategists, so we should stop expecting them to do something they can't – or don't want to – do. If you want real strategic technology leverage, find people who live and breathe it free from the distractions of operational technology. These are not jobs easily combined.

REMINDER #5: EMERGING TECHNOLOGIES

There's a ton of emerging technologies you need to understand at the functional level. If you don't track and define these technologies, you will fail. There are three questions about each technology you must answer: What it is? Why you should care? What you should do about it? Examples? Reduce the number of programmers on your team and replace them with low-code jockeys; slow-roll quantum; stop taking the metaverse seriously; and stop doing multi-cloud.

REMINDER #6: DIGITAL TRANSFORMATION ISN'T ALWAYS TRANSFORMATIVE

Stop over-selling digital transformation. Companies define everything as "transformation". Disruptive transformation – where processes and business models are fundamentally changed – is rare. Stop chasing it and stop selling it. Besides, if you don't have deep process inventories, you have no transformation chance anyway.

REMINDER #7: AI AND MACHINE LEARNING ARE FOR REAL

AI and machine learning are game changers. You'd better understand them. If you don't, you will fail. Way too many companies have too little respect for what AI and machine learning can do. Don't be one of them.

REMINDER #8: TECHNOLOGY POLICY IS FOR SALE

Ignore technology policy at your own risk — remember it's for sale through the highest paid lobbyist. Decide if you want to directly influence policy or react to policies influenced by others – and invest accordingly. Sitting on the sidelines is unacceptable.

REMINDER #9: FLAT ORGANISATIONAL STRUCTURES FAIL REMOTE MANAGEMENT

Flat organisations are horrible for managing distributed organisations (managed remotely). Focus on hierarchies, accountability, work-products and no-emotion leadership. Stop trying to please everyone with flat structures, especially when you can't even see them.

REMINDER #10: FAILURE IS HUMAN

You also fail because you don't have the right talent performing the right tasks at the right time for the right money. All new recruiting and retention strategies are necessary. It's time to plan an off-site with your HR team about how to fill the competency gaps all over your company – because they're there.

There are more than ten reasons why enterprise technology fails. You can probably list ten more. So, why do they never seem to go away? Why are we so accepting of, for example, missing strategies, models and processes? Why do we stress over commoditised operational technology and so little about strategic differentiation enabled by emerging technology? Why don't we deal with the talent crisis upstairs, downstairs and next door? (Is that why there are so many consultants?)

Is it time to look in the mirror? No – skip that step. We've already tried it. The argument that might compel changes is purely financial. Do you know how much money you could save, and how much revenue you could generate, if you just stopped the bleeding?

STRATEGIC ELEMENTS AND PROCESSES

Your strategic technology plan can be as straightforward as you want it to be. This is not rocket science. Look at Figure 23. Note the left side of the figure – which defines your strategic technology game plan.

There are three major steps:

1. Develop a strategy (comprising business objectives, develop a business model and business processes).
2. Track and match emerging technologies with as-is and to-be processes.
3. Prototype the most promising matches.

Note the middle of Figure 23, which lists the steps you should take on your way toward improved/automated/eliminated/reinvented processes, a competitive business model and a new business strategy. They provide context. The outcomes are on the right side of Figure 23.

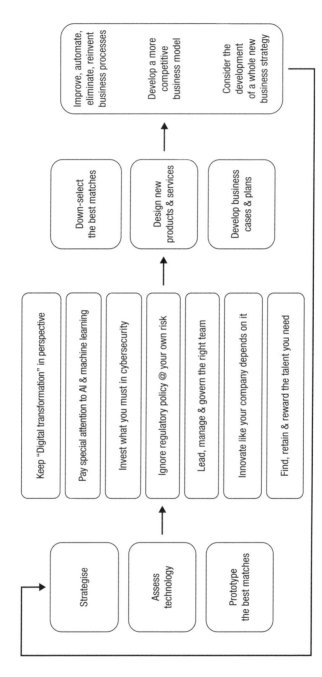

Figure 23 A strategic technology game plan

STRATEGY, TECHNOLOGY AND PROTOTYPES

Strategic thinking is a core competency: if you can't strategise, you can't inform your business model, the processes that comprise the model, or technologies that will improve, automate, eliminate or invent competitive processes. I'm not sure how many times I have to say this: much of the failure of strategic technology planning is traceable to how much you outsource strategic activities. No matter how hard they sell you, how well they dress or how many clients they have, they can never understand your business processes better than you. Nor should they ever be able to understand the technologies most likely to impact those processes.

What do you need to do? Here are the steps:

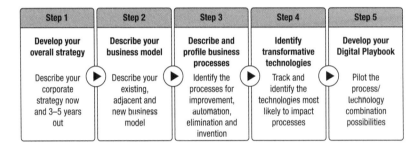

Figure 24 Five strategic steps

Your strategy will be converted into your business model and your business model will yield the processes you're trying to improve, automate, eliminate or reinvent with existing and emerging technology. How? First and foremost, remember your core competencies:

Build your business strategy around objectives, scope and competitive advantage:

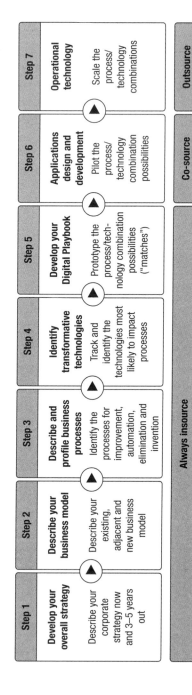

Figure 25 Business-technology core competencies

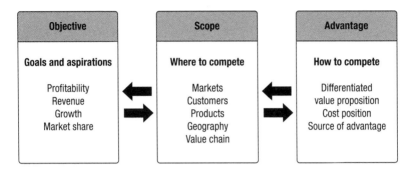

Figure 26 Elements of your business strategy
Adapted from *Corporate Strategy: A Resource-Based Approach* by David J. Collis and Cynthia A. Montgomery.

Next, identify and define the business processes that define your business model.

Each element of the business model canvas is composed of existing processes that together describe how you do what you do. They're also the source of new processes. If you can't describe your business model, you can't identify existing processes in need of improvement, automation, elimination, or any new processes that, when partnered with the right technology, might improve your competitive position in the market.

Pick one platform – BPM (business process modelling with its notation [BPMN]) – and then pick one BPMN software tool and standardise it throughout your company – no exceptions.

Investments in (1) strategy, (2) business modelling and (3) BPM[3] are no-brainers: if you cannot define your strategy, your business model and the "as-is" and "to-be" processes that make you competitive, then the game is lost before it begins.

An example of a (loan approval/rejection) business process model (with notation) is in Figure 27.

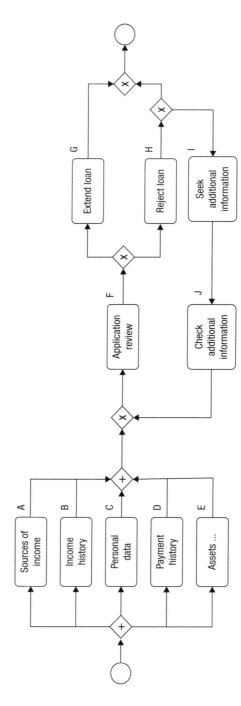

Figure 27 The loan approval/rejection process

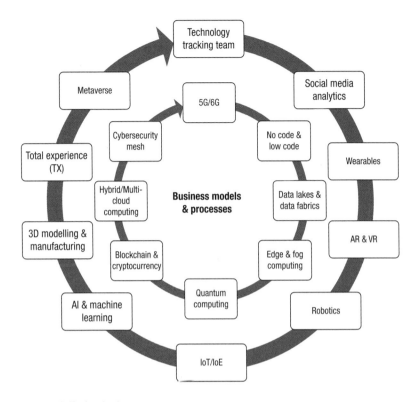

Figure 28 Technologies

You also need to track the technologies that can impact your business processes, as shown in Figure 28.

You need a team of in-house professionals – full-time employees – to identify and track the technologies most likely to impact your business.

You need discipline around the technology assessment process designed to vet technology impact upon current and future business models and processes and answer a simple question: *"Will this technology help us make money, save money, or both?" "What processes will it improve, automate, eliminate or reinvent?*

Figure 29 describes the relationship between processes and technologies. Note that this too is a two-way arrangement, where the processes link to as-is and to-be processes and vice versa.

Process/technology leverage? First, identify the processes that take the most time, cost you the most money and are the most amenable to technology disruption (or at least change). (You should already have this list via your

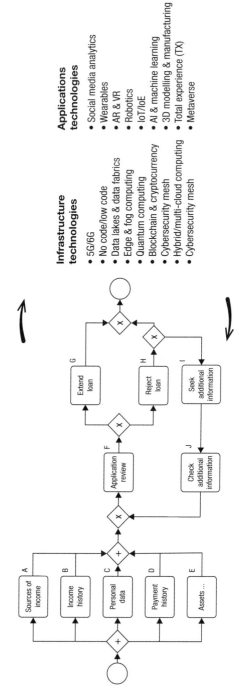

Infrastructure technologies

- 5G/6G
- No code/low code
- Data lakes & data fabrics
- Edge & fog computing
- Quantum computing
- Blockchain & cryptocurrency
- Cybersecurity mesh
- Hybrid/multi-cloud computing
- Cybersecurity mesh

Applications technologies

- Social media analytics
- Wearables
- AR & VR
- Robotics
- IoT/IoE
- AI & machine learning
- 3D modelling & manufacturing
- Total experience (TX)
- Metaverse

Figure 29 Emerging technologies for process improvement, automation, elimination and reinvention

process mining activities.) Figure 27, for example, models the loan approval/rejection process. Which of the sub-processes could be improved, automated, eliminated or completely reimagined? Which technologies "match" with each of the improve/automate, eliminate or completely re-imagine objectives? How might the processes and sub-processes around loans be improved, automated, eliminated or completely reimagined? Which technologies could yield such outcomes? It's the same for the lender: which technologies could improve, automate, eliminate or completely reimagine the loan approval/rejection processes and sub-processes?

Hypotheses should be generated, such as "machine learning can automate huge chunks of the loan process." Or "data gathering can be enabled by augmented analytics." These hypotheses can then be tested with prototypes designed to assess just how impactful the process/technology matches might be, as suggested in Figure 30.

Matching and prototyping are two plays that will help you win. They're the "go-to" plays you should execute all the time. Perhaps now you understand why I'm so dogmatic about core competencies. Leverage comes from a deep understanding of business processes and a wide understanding of existing and emerging digital technology. No one can understand your business better than your team. Your team must also understand technology to identify the most potentially impactful process/technology matches. Outsourcing the matching process to consultants is a mistake for so many reasons. It's that simple. If you don't have a team that can match processes and technologies, build one. But don't default to consultants who have half-baked ideas about how your industry works, where it's going, who you are, who you most dangerous competitors are, what you do and what you need to succeed.

Can you really tell me they can do all this better than you?

CONTEXT

DIGITAL TRANSFORMATION

The process/technology matching/prototyping process is a core competency. In order to optimise that competency, a number of things should be true. For example, while the whole world is obsessed with "digital transformation", you should keep it in perspective by dispelling the myths that surround massive annual investments in transformation. Make sure you identify your transformation target because they all have different qualities, risks and impact. Remember that so-called "disruptive" transformation is hard and risky, and incremental transformation is safe but boring. Who do you want to be?

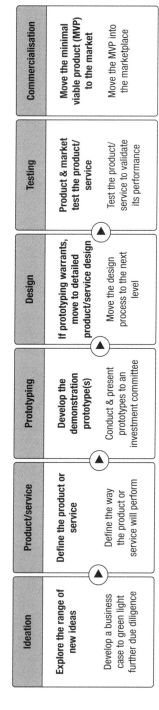

Figure 30 Stage-gating

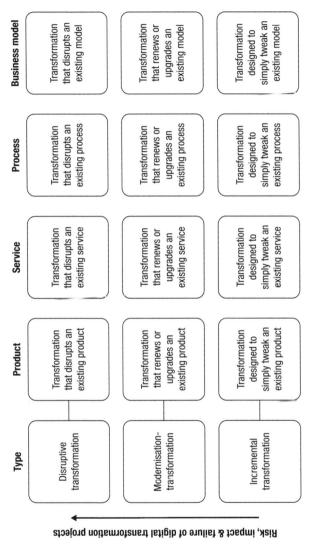

Figure 31 The type, impact and risks of digital transformation projects

AI AND MACHINE LEARNING

There are lots of technologies you should track. They're all over *The Digital Playbook*. But there's one family you'd better track especially closely because it has the greatest potential impact on your business processes. Of course I'm talking about AI and machine learning. Why? Because the range of applications is staggering, including all the vertical industries and the models and businesses that enable them. AI will profoundly impact healthcare, transportation, accounting, finance, manufacturing, customer service, aviation, education, sales, marketing, law, entertainment, media, security, negotiation, war and peace. No industry or process is safe from the impact that AI – across all of its components – will have in the shortrun and especially over the next seven to ten years. Keep in mind also that AI will integrate across business and technology architectures, databases and applications.

Automation is the objective; here's the plan (see Figure 32):

Note how the ten-step process leverages business processes and process mining.

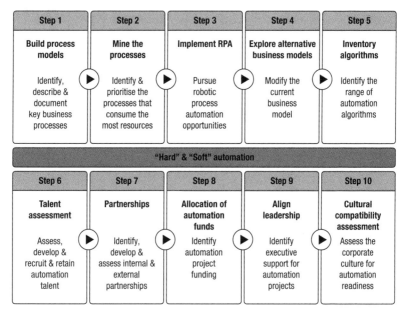

Step 1	Step 2	Step 3	Step 4	Step 5
Build process models	**Mine the processes**	**Implement RPA**	**Explore alternative business models**	**Inventory algorithms**
Identify, describe & document key business processes	Identify & prioritise the processes that consume the most resources	Pursue robotic process automation opportunities	Modify the current business model	Identify the range of automation algorithms

"Hard" & "Soft" automation

Step 6	Step 7	Step 8	Step 9	Step 10
Talent assessment	**Partnerships**	**Allocation of automation funds**	**Align leadership**	**Cultural compatibility assessment**
Assess, develop & recruit & retain automation talent	Identify, develop & assess internal & external partnerships	Identify automation project funding	Identify executive support for automation projects	Assess the corporate culture for automation readiness

Figure 32 Ten steps to automation
From Andriole and *IEEE IT Professional*.
Andriole, SJ (2022) "Automation is a 10-Step Competitive Necessity." Published in: IEEE IT Professional (Volume: 24, Issue: 1, 01 Jan. Feb. 2022) DOI: 10.1109/MITP.2021.3136017

CYBERSECURITY

The number and severity of cyberattacks will grow because cyberwarfare is a cost-effective solution to all sorts of problems – and opportunities: cyberwarfare is a revenue stream, a new business model, a weapon and digital transformation with its own unique flavour. The whole world is warning anyone who will listen about cyberwarfare. Why? Because it's the cheapest, easiest, fastest and most effective form of warfare we've ever seen, and because cyberwarfare defences are more vulnerable than they've ever been.

It's important to embrace industry best practices at least "for show". You must embrace the best practices required of your industry regardless of how effective they might be in securing your networks, databases and applications. You must satisfy your auditors and partners.

You should understand that the consequences of breaches and other attacks are not as impactful as they might be. Consequently, companies – maybe yours – may underinvest in cybersecurity with some level of impunity. Remember:

> "*Money alone is probably not the answer,* as higher cybersecurity spending did not necessarily translate into a higher maturity level'* . . . there was not a strong correlation between those that spent a lot and the maturity ratings achieved.*"

REGULATORY POLICY

You have to track the regulations that affect your business. The shortlist is in Figure 33.

Are there other areas? Absolutely. Track all of the areas relevant to your existing and future business models. Regulatory policy is all around you. Some focuses on the structure of the technology industry – like oligarchies – and some focuses on specific issues – like privacy. Some policies focus on infrastructure – like Internet for All – and some on specific technologies – like AI and machine learning. You should see policy as a threat and an opportunity. You should also seize opportunities to influence policy. Sitting on the sidelines is not an option.

LEAD, MANAGE AND GOVERN THE RIGHT TEAM

"Internal consultants" can implement the brains versus brawn directive. Teams of consultants can be formed and anointed to perform many of the tasks traditional consultants perform. Reduce the number of "chiefs" at your company. Resist the industry's desire to create new functions, budgets, and silos. Keep it simple.

Remember that specialisation in a converging world is misguided. The number of approved, licensed chiefs you have explains your level of organisational complexity: the more chiefs, the more complex your business

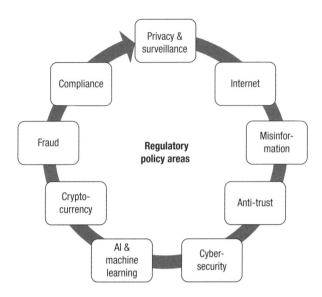

Figure 33 Regulatory policy areas

structures, rules and processes. Chiefs increase organisation autonomy, atrophy and dysfunction. The more you have, the more confusion and conflict there will be. Organise hierarchically; avoid flat management structures, especially as you try to assign and track remote work. Consider RACI charts to remove ambiguity. Fear, confusion, optimism, uncertainty, denial and worse are driving some of the most expensive operational and strategic technology decisions you can make. Try to identify them and minimise their impact. Pay very serious attention to the importance of governance, which is about rules, roles, relationships and ways of working. Remember that ambiguity is your lifelong enemy: the more ambiguity around rules, roles, relationships and ways of working at your company, the less productive you will be. Finally, note that governance only works when it's enforced.

INNOVATE

Always innovate for purpose. You innovate to reduce costs and increase profitable revenue – not because it's fun, or because your mad scientists in the basement have killer ideas just waiting to be freed. Remember that innovation is not commercialisation. Innovation enables commercialisation – not the other way around.

"Innovation" is the matrix in Figure 34.

Here's the innovation $\longrightarrow$ commercialisation process you should adopt (Figure 35):

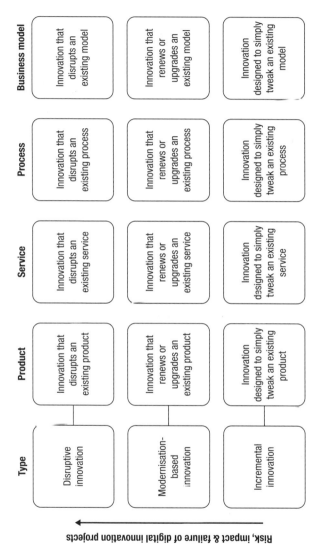

Figure 34 Targets of innovation

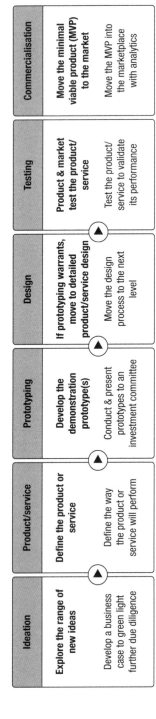

Figure 35 Innovation – commercialisation

Business cases to launch innovation projects bound for commercialisation should be simple.

FIND, RETAIN AND REWARD THE TALENT YOU NEED

You should routinely perform "work force analyses" to measure the gap between the business-technology expertise you need and what you have on staff. Make sure your team has expertise in five areas:

1. Business strategy, models and processes.
2. Disruptive technologies.
3. Pilots.
4. Cloud delivery.
5. Strategic management.

You should rank-order the first and second areas – (1) business strategy/ models/ processes and (2) disruptive technologies – higher than the other three. AI and machine learning, including the algorithms that make them smart, should be designated special talent requirements. You also need talent in privacy and surveillance, misinformation/disinformation, diversity, inclusion and equality and people management. You must pursue as many recruitment channels and pipelines as possible, including relationships with universities, search firms, former employees and the technology associations that advance the skills and competencies you need. Retention should include conventional and unconventional approaches. Respect, segmented performance recognition and flexibility should be added to retention strategies. Rewards should be chiefly financial, sprinkled with some rewards suggested by your superstars.

OUTCOMES

There are three outcomes you should seek:

1. A prioritised list of improved, automated, eliminated and reinvented business processes validated by stage-gated prototyping.
2. Informed by these processes, the development of a modified or new business model.

3. Should the prioritised processes and revised business model warrant, the development of a whole new business model (and even an entire business strategy, if the business model looks weak).

Ultimately, *The Digital Playbook* is about competitiveness. The scope of competitiveness depends upon the talent and efforts of your team – not the process described here.

The three outcomes listed above constitute your business-technology strategy, which is ever-changing: the strategy you develop today will yield to tomorrow's events. Note, for example, how "The Great Resignation" has impacted process/technology matches. Resignations have triggered an increase in automation spending, especially in labour-intensive industries.

The strategic technology elements, steps and processes described here remain the same. Your job is to continuously improve, automate, eliminate and reinvent the processes that enable your business strategy through your business model.

The percentage of processes you reinvent will determine the likelihood of a new business model – and accelerated competitiveness. Disruption – so long as it's well-conceived – is the essence of competitiveness. If there's enough disruption, your whole business model – even your overall strategy – may change, which is the ultimate competitive pivot. The appetite to pursue disruptive process change that will change your business model and business strategy is an accessible behaviour. In other words, you can be as disruptive as you want to be. The methodology described here is a competitive weapon you can use for target practice or to attack your industry. It's really up to you.

AFTERTHOUGHTS

In spite of all of the misinformation and disinformation out there, facts still matter.

Does anyone remember Joe Friday from the ancient US TV series *Dragnet*? I certainly didn't, but when I heard the phrase "Just the facts, ma'am" recently, I looked him up. Turns out that this 1950s fictional detective always got right to the point. For those who care – and I suspect there aren't many of you – Dragnet (Mikkelson, 2022):

"Started out as a radio drama in 1949, made the transition to television in 1951 (and aired in both media simultaneously through 1957), became a feature film in 1954, spawned a revival TV series and made-for-TV movie in 1966, was spoofed in a 1987 movie starring Dan

Akroyd and Tom Hanks, and was spun off yet again (after Webb's death) as a new syndicated series in 1989." (This Joe Friday guy – AKA Jack Webb – had quite a run.)

Joe Friday is attributed to have said – apparently frequently to female witnesses – *"Just the facts, ma'am."* Aside from the obvious implied sexism, which haunts twentieth-century media, Joe Friday never actually said *"just the facts, ma'am"*, though he said things similar enough to segue to the issue at hand: facts. In this case, facts – *data* – about technology and its financial relationship to the company it serves.

I won't name names, but I will tell you that a large number of CIOs, CTOs, CEOs, COOs and now CDOs I've worked with over the years, for some reason, couldn't answer the most basic financial questions about their technology spending and the impact it's having on their strategy, not to mention the strategic reasons why it even exists.

Is there something especially hard about the questions? Nope.

Here are the apparently mysterious questions you need to answer reflexively:

- *What's the company's business strategy?*

    We've talked a lot about strategy in *The Digital Playbook*. If executives don't understand the business strategy, they cannot optimise technology. Period. Way too many cannot describe their own company's strategy. I only wish I could name names here. I really do. (But, on second thought, I like my life.) A recent encounter resulted in the CEO saying to his direct reports upon learning that no one could produce even a single piece of paper that describes the business strategy, *"Well, I think we all know what the strategy is, right?"*

- *What's the business model?*

    Most – that's *most* – executives cannot describe the business model of their companies. That's right, they don't know how they make money, who they directly or indirectly compete with (or the status of the competitors), who their key partners are, the key processes, etc. They could not fill out the business model canvas with any precision.

- *What are the business processes that define how we work?*

    It's obviously important to know which processes define a company, which processes are the most challenging and which are under review for improvement, replacement, automation, elimination or reinvention. But they almost always fail to list them.

- *What's the business-technology strategy?*

  In an all-digital time, it's important to understand the relationship between technology – especially emerging technology – and the business strategy, model and processes that literally are the circulatory system of a company. But they cannot.

How about ground level? Are things any better? Here are the in-the-trenches questions you'd expect executives to nail every time:

- *How much money is spent on technology every year?*

  It's important to know the total amount and the relative allocations across the categories – hardware, software, communications, support, consultants, etc. – but also across categories of special importance to your company and your industry, like privacy and security in the financial services industry and supply-chain planning and management in the manufacturing and distribution industries. These days, it's also important to understand – in some detail – exactly how much and where money is spent on AI, machine learning, regardless of the industry.

- *What percentage of revenue is spent on operational and strategic technology?*

  The numbers here are important to determine if you're an operational spender obsessed with managing costs, or if you're a strategic spender seeking competitive advantage from your investments in digital technology. Companies that spend their gross revenue on total technology investments per year in their industry tend to be operationally focused, that is, on managing technology as a cost centre. If the people in your organisation wax poetic about how they look to technology for strategic advantage, but spend less than the industry percentage, they're delusional. Companies that spend more than their industry brethren are generally strategic investors. The key metric here is how spending-by-industry varies. Variations within industries are insightful (Computer Economics, 2022). Some industries spend less than 8 per cent of revenue on technology, while others – software and cloud industries – spend much more.

  The important metric is where a company lies across industry averages (Weins, 2020): software companies (25 per cent of revenue), cloud companies (16 per cent), financial services companies (10 per cent), services companies (7 per cent), retail/ecommerce companies (6 per cent), consumer products companies (6 per cent), transportation and logistics companies (5 per cent), healthcare companies (5 per cent) and industrial products companies (4 per cent). Where is your company along these industry averages?

- *What are direct, adjacent and indirect competitors spending?*

If your competitors are spending twice what you and your industry brethren are spending it could mean several things. Perhaps you're spending too little, or perhaps they're spending way too much. Competitive intelligence is worth every penny you spend. You must know what they're spending, how they're spending it and their spending trends. Again, segmentation is your insightful friend.

- *How much of the technology budget is discretionary vs non-discretionary?*

Is there any freedom in your budget? If the boss came in and asked for $500k for a strategic project, would you be able to find the money? Or $100k for a tactical one? Is most of the annual technology budget already accounted for, or is there some room for special projects, pilots, etc.? So-called entrepreneurial programmes are often underfunded in small discretionary budgets. Financial agility is an asset, especially given the volatility of digital technology.

- *What's the return on the operational and strategic technology investments?*

It's important to know the total cost of applications, communications, cloud, etc. in order to understand where the money goes and how impactful it is. Here are the top three spending priorities across industries (Weins, 2020): digital transformation (54 per cent), cybersecurity (49 per cent) and cloud-first/cloud migration (40 per cent).

This is modelling heaven for lots of the friends and foes in your orbit. ROI calculations are necessary evils of all budgeting processes. If you don't measure ROI – with explicit operational *and* business metrics – then it will be impossible to quantify the impact of your technology spending. If there's no standard ROI methodology, then you should – along with the financial professionals at your company – develop one. What's the ROI of your spending in digital transformation, cybersecurity and cloud-first/cloud migration?

■ *How good are the technology leaders?*

This is perhaps the hardest question on the list. Not because the data itself is hard to find, but because the overall ROI is likely to be poor – or worse. If that's the case, then there's definitely some blame blowback onto the team. Put another way, if the annual ROI is poor, it's time to replace the team, though most companies are loathe to take this somewhat obvious step for all sorts of personal and professional reasons.

Once you get the answers to these questions, put them in a dashboard for everyone to see – unless, of course, the answers are – well – not what you think everyone should see (which is a problem unto itself). If the data's hard to find or, worse, explain, consider why that's the case. Chances are "technology" is not a first (second or third) spending priority. It's also – as suggested just moments ago – often a hands-off area. If the data reveals poor trends, data-driven solutions are in plain view. So, maybe the first line of defence is to scramble the data so no one can see how bad things really are. Otherwise, all of this data would be on the tips of everyone's tongue. Of course, it's always possible that data poverty exists because companies have bad internal analytics, or their dashboards are bad. It's possible that no one's ever linked spending trends with operational or strategic efficiency. Yes, it's possible, but incredibly unlikely unless everyone's gone back in time before data-driven management was a thing. But who knows how many executives are still living in the twentieth century? Anyone come to mind? (God, I wish I could name names.)

In any case, these are the questions to which answers should be obvious. If you can't answer them, then reread *The Digital Playbook.*

THE FINAL (REALLY, REALLY IMPORTANT) REQUIREMENT: MANAGE THE CRAZIES

Let's just all agree that the elephants in the room are actually people, the people you work with every day. But let's also acknowledge that there's a resistance to see the elephants or deal with the often-obvious steps necessary to solve real "people problems". As the pace of technology accelerates, digital competition explodes, and the need for effective leadership grows, companies must revisit and reimagine how it recruits, rewards and manages their technology teams – including especially leadership.

Let's get some help with this.

Occam's Razor (Britannica, 2022) states *"that 'plurality should not be posited without necessity.' The principle gives precedence to simplicity: of two competing theories, the simpler explanation of an entity is to be preferred. The principle is also expressed as 'entities are not to be multiplied beyond necessity.'"* There are similar principles out there, notably the "KISS" principle – keep it simple, stupid – which "most likely finds its origins in similar minimalist concepts, such as Occam's Razor", Leonardo da Vinci's "simplicity is the ultimate sophistication", Shakespeare's "brevity is the soul of wit", Mies van der Rohe's "less is more", Bjarne Stroustrup's "make simple tasks simple!", or Antoine de Saint-Exupéry's "it seems that perfection is reached not when there is nothing left to add, but when there is nothing left to take away". Colin Chapman, the founder of *Lotus Cars*, urged his designers to "simplify, then add lightness". Heath Robinson's and Rube Goldberg's machines, intentionally overly-complex solutions to simple tasks or problems, are humorous examples of "non-KISS" solutions, including Einstein's "make everything as simple as possible, but not simpler".

Is any of this getting through?

When it comes to strategic technology, we insist on attributing failure to anything and everything but the obvious. We want to believe things that have no basis in fact – or even reality. Like the earth is flat, Covid vaccines make us magnetic and left-wing American democrats consume babies. On the not-quite-as-crazy list are what *tens of millions* of Americans actually believe (H., 2015) such as:

- *"About 30% of Americans believe that climate change is mainly caused by 'natural changes in the environment.'" (Yale/Gallup/Clearvision Poll)*
- *"10% of Americans think it's the environmentalists themselves who cause devastating oil spills. (Public Policy Polling)*
- *"18% of Americans believe that the Earth is the center of the universe. (Gallup Poll)*
- *"A quarter of Americans think the Darwin's theory of evolution is not real. (Pew Research Report)*
- *"Almost 33% of Americans believe in ghosts and 18% of Americans even claim they have seen some. (Pew Research Report)*

- *"More than three quarters of Americans believe there are indisputable evidences that aliens have already visited our planet. (National Geographic Survey)*
- *"26% of Americans still believe in witchcraft. (Gallup Poll)*
- *"Almost a quarter of Americans believe in reincarnation (i.e., they are convinced they were once another person). (Pew Research Report)*
- *"15% of American voters believe that the media adds secret mind controlling technology to TV broadcasts. (Public Policy Polling)*
- *"20% believe that cellphones cause cancer but that the government is afraid of large corporations and refuses to address the health hazard. (University of Chicago Study.)"*

What's the point of all this "stupidity"?

*It's important to understand – **to know** – that many of the same people who believe these (and many other things) run projects, companies and government agencies. Many of the people who believe these things are **technology** consultants, run **technology** companies and manage **technology** projects.* (Do you think any of them run government **technology** agencies?)

To assume otherwise defies Occam's core principle – and other commonsense notions of likelihoods, not to mention any statistical measures of probability. Asked differently, what's the probability that *none* of the believers of *any* of these crazy things run technology companies, manage technology projects or consult? Zero.

It gets worse.

When we delve into the psychological profiles of many of our friends, associates, vendors, consultants and leaders, it gets horrifyingly messy. What's the probability that *none* of the people in your professional orbit believe *any* less-than-factual things and have *no* personality challenges (or outright disorders)? Zero.

I started this analysis a while ago when I attempted to explain why so many technology projects fail (Andriole, 2012). I offered that it was all about the people all the time, and that the lack of the right talent, poor executive support and anti-technology corporate cultures explained more about failure than the old favourites, like scope creep, requirements mismanagement, etc. It's the long way of saying that incompetent people with strange world views (and other traits) can be damaging to strategic success. Who knew? *Everyone* – and that's the elephant in the room so few of us are willing to see. How many people do you know who have no business doing what they're doing? I stopped counting years ago. William of Ockham had it right: the simplest explanation is usually the best. We just refuse to accept it.

THE DIGITAL PLAYBOOK

I gave you the ability to develop a really solid strategic technology plan, a plan that will make you competitive as we all march toward an all-digital world.

But you need to keep the crazies as far away from it as you can.

Remember that everything in *The Digital Playbook* is doable.

The plays work.

You can win.

I promise.

REFERENCES

9Lenses (2022) "Internal versus External Consulting – Advantages and Disadvantages", 9Lenses, https://9lenses.com/internal-versus-external-consulting-advantages-and-disadvantages/?s

Alexander, Donovan (2021) "9 Robots That Are Invading The Agriculture Industry", *Interesting Engineering.*

Alton, Larry (2020) "The 8 Best Cybersecurity Strategies for Small Businesses in 2021", *Inc. Magazine.*

Andriole, Stephen J. (2017) "Five Myths of Digital Transformation", *Sloan Management Review.*

Andriole, Stephen J. (2012) "IT's All About the People." CRC Press.

Andriole, Stephen, J. (2022) https://andriole.com.

Andriole, Stephen J., *Forbes,* https://www.forbes.com/sites/steveandriole/?sh=3deccc051c88.

Armstrong, Annie (2022) "Looks Like the Auction of Melania Trump's First NFT Was Such a Dud She Had to Buy the Thing Herself", ArtNet News.

Authenticity Consulting (2020) "Field Guide to Consulting and Organizational Development", Authenticity Consulting, https://managementhelp.org/consulting/int-ext-consultants.pdf.

Aysha, M. (2020) "Porsche on the Use of Additive Manufacturing", 3Dnatives.

Baral, Susmita (2021) "When Will Automation Take Over the Trucking Industry?", LA Times Blog.

Barnhart, Brent (2021) "10 of the Best Social Media Analytics Tools for Marketers", Sprout Social.

Bischoff, P. (2021) "How Data Breaches Affect Stock Market Share Prices." Comparitech. https://www.comparitech.com/blog/information-security/data-breach-share-price-analysis/

Bobrow, Adam (2022) "Does Spending More on Cyber Mean Less Risk?", Foresight Resilience Strategies.

BookAuthority (2022) "100 Best Business Strategy Books of All Time".

Britannica (2022) "Robotics Technology", https://www.britannica.com/technology/robotics.

Brooks, Ryan (2020) "Compliance Tools: Choosing the Right Solutions", Netwrix.

Bughin, Jacques, Catlin, Tanguy, Hirt, Martin and Willmott, Paul (2018) "Why Digital Strategies Fail", *McKinsey Quarterly.*

Carmichael, Doug (2018) "Audit vs. Fraud Examination", *CPA Journal.*

Carucci, Ron (2017) "Executives Fail to Execute Strategy Because They're Too Internally Focused", *Harvard Business Review.*

CFI Team (2020) "Business Strategy vs Business Model: Learn About the Differences", Corporate Finance Institute (CFI).

CFI Team (2022) "Threat of New Entrants", Corporate Finance Institute (CFI).

Chai, Wesley (2022) "Cloud Computing", TechTarget.

Changing Minds (2017) "The Elements of the Conversation", Changing Minds, http://changingminds.org/techniques/conversation/elements/elements.htm.

Christensen, Clayton (1997) *"The Innovator's Dilemma",* Harvard University Press.

CMTC (2021) "Advanced Manufacturing, Additive Manufacturing, Future of Manufacturing: Top 8 Industries Benefiting from Additive Manufacturing".

Collis, David J. and Montgomery, Cynthia A. (2005) *"Corporate Strategy: A Resource-Based Approach"*, Boston: McGraw-Hill/Irwin.

Comply Advantage (2022) "Cryptocurrency Regulations in the United States", Comply Advantage.

Computer Economics (2022) "IT Spending as a Percentage of Revenue by Industry, Company Size, and Region", Computer Economics.

Cone, Edward (2022) "Blame Enough to Go Around at K-Mart", *Baseline.*

Consultancy-me (2022) "External vs Internal Consultants", Consultancy-me, https://www.consultancy-me.com/consulting-industry/external-vs-internal-consultants

Davenport, Thomas H. and Spanyi, Andrew (2019) "What Process Mining Is, and Why Companies Should Do It", *Harvard Business Review.*

Deloitte (2022) "The Role of Culture in Digital Transformation", *CIO Journal.*

DeMuro, Jonas P. (2019) "What is Container Technology?", *TechRadar*.

Department of Homeland Security (2018) "Cybersecurity Strategy", Department of Homeland Security.

Devaney, Erik (2022) "9 Types of Organizational Structure Every Company Should Consider", HubSpot.

DFRLab (2017) "#BotSpot: Twelve Ways to Spot a Bot", DFRLab.

Digital Guide Ionos (2022) "Social Bots – the Technology Behind Fake News", Digital Guide Ionos.

Dugan, Regina E. and Gabriel, Kaigham J. (2013) "'Special Forces'" Innovation: How DARPA Attacks Problems", *Harvard Business Review*.

Duke Health (2022) "Lobbying Definitions, Exceptions, and Examples", Duke Health.

Eide, Naomi (2021) "4 Predictions for CIOs to Watch from Gartner", CIO Dive.

Embroker Team (2022) "How Much Can a Data Breach Cost Your Business?", Embroker.

The Enterprisers Project (2016) "What is Digital Transformation?".

FBI (2022) "White-Collar Crime", FBI.

FDIC (2022) "FDIC Law, Regulations, Related Acts", FDIC.

FinTech Futures (2013) "Goldman Sachs Trading Error is 'A Warning to All'".

Fortune Business Insights (2021) "Virtual Reality (VR) in Gaming Market to Reach USD 53.44 Billion by 2028".

Franck, Thomas (2021) "Fidelity to Launch Bitcoin ETF as Investment Giant Builds its Digital Asset Business", CNBC.

Frankenfield, Jake (2021) "Quantum Computing", Investopedia.

Frey, Carl and Osborne, Michael (2013) "The Future of Employment: How Susceptible are Jobs to Computerisation", University of Oxford.

Galer, Susan (2018) "Build Intelligent Bots in Three Minutes: SAP Intelligent Robotic Process Automation", SAP News.

Gartner Group (2022a) "Cybersecurity Mesh", https://www.gartner.com/en/information-technology/trends/.

GeeksforGeeks (2022) "Difference Between IoE and IoT".

General Electric (2022) "What is Additive Manufacturing?".

Ghosh, Pallab (2018) "AI Early Diagnosis Could Save Heart & Cancer Patients", BBC News.

Greyling, Cobus (2020) "Key Considerations in Designing A Conversational User Interface", Medium.

The Guardian (2021) "US Amazon Web Services Outage Hits Netflix, Slack, Ring and Doordash".

H, Petr (2015) "25 Unbelievable Things Americans Believe", List25.

Hayes, Adam (2022a) "Wearable Technology", Investopedia.

Hayes, Adam (2022b) "What is Blockchain?", Investopedia.

Hayworth, Suzanna (2018) "Create a Responsibility Assignment Matrix (RACI Chart) that Works", *Digital Project Manager.*

Hill, Michael (2022) "What is the Cost of a Data Breach?", CSO, https://www.csoonline.com/article/3434601/what-is-the-cost-of-a-data-breach.html.

Hill, Michael and Swinhoe, Dan (2021) "The 15 Biggest Data Breaches of the 21st Century", CSO.

Honeywell (2021) "Why Companies Say Automation is a Top Goal".

Humanperf Blog (2021) "Will the Total Experience (TX) be the Key Trend for the Coming Decade?".

IBM. (2022) Ponemon Institute Cost of a Data Breach Report. https://www.ibm.com/downloads/cas/3R8N1DZJ

IBM Cloud Education (2020) "Supervised Learning", IBM.

Information Management (2016) Slideshow, https://www.information-management.com/slideshow/10-lessons-learned-from-2016s-biggest-data-breaches.

Insight (2022) "Cybersecurity Mesh", https://www.insight.com/en_US/glossary/c/cybersecurity-mesh.html.

The Investopedia Team (2022) "Porter's 5 Forces", Investopedia.

Jibilian, Isabella and Canales, Katie (2021) "The US is Readying Sanctions Against Russia Over the SolarWinds Cyber Attack", *Insider.*

Julie (2018) "8 Rater Biases that are Impacting your Performance Management", TrakStar.

Kennedy, Joe (2018) "We're No. 25: Why the US Must Increase Its Tax Incentives for R&D", Industry Week.

Kim, Paul (2022) "What are the Environmental Impacts of Cryptocurrencies?", *Insider.*

Knight, Will (2018) "China Wants to Shape the Global Future of Artificial Intelligence", *MIT Technology Review.*

LawGeex (2017) "Comparing the Performance of Artificial Intelligence to Human Lawyers in the Review of Standard Business Contracts", LawGeex.

Lee, Kai-Fu (2020) "The Third Revolution in Warfare", The Atlantic.

Levy, Steven (2021) "AR Is Where the Real Metaverse Is Going to Happen", *Wired Magazine.*

Luksza, Kamila (2018) "Bot Traffic Is Bigger Than Human", Voluum.

Manning, Ellen (2018) "Could Emotionally Intelligent Bots Help Build Trust Between Man & Machine?", World Economic Forum.

Markuson, Daniel (2020) "NordVPN Completes Advanced Application Security Audit", NordVPV.

Marquet, Kristin (2022) "Six Ways to Retain Your Best Talent", *Fast Company.*

McKinsey (2022) "Tech Talent Tectonics: Ten New Realities for Finding, Keeping, & Developing Talent", https://www.mckinsey.com/capabilities/mckinsey-digital/our-insights/tech-talent-tectonics-ten-new-realities-for-finding-keeping-and-developing-talent.

Melnick, Kyle (2021) "Someone Spent $450K To Be Snoop Dogg's Neighbor in The Metaverse", VK Scout.

Mikkelson, David (2022) "Dragnet: 'Just the Facts. Ma'am'", Snopes.

Molla, Rani (2019) "Visa Approvals for Tech Workers are on the Decline", Vox.

Montgomery, Olivia and Kumar, Rahul (2020) "What Is a RACI Chart?", Software Advice.

Morrow, Emily (2021) "Total experience: Definition, Benefits, Tips of TX", The Future of Customer Engagement & Experience.

Narayanaswamy, Krishna (2017) "Ensuring That the Next Big Data Breach Isn't Yours", *Information Management.*

NetApp (2022) "What is a Data Fabric?".

Oladimeji, Saheed and Kerner, Sean Michael (2022) "SolarWinds Hack Explained: Everything You Need to Know", WhatIs.com.

Olavsrud, Thor and Boulton, Clint (2022) "What is RPA? A Revolution in Business Process Automation", *CIO Magazine.*

Openresearch.amsterdam (2021) "What is Artificial Intelligence?", Redactie openresearch.amsterdam.

O'Shaughnessy, Kim (2016) "8 Reasons Why ERP is Important", SelectHub.

Overheid, Andrew (2022) "Understanding Fog Computing vs Edge Computing", Onlogic Blog.

Palmer, Shelly (2018) "How to Build Your Own Troll Bot Army", Shellypalmer.com.

Pratt, Mary (2021) "Low-Code & No-Code Development Platforms", TechTarget.

Pratt, Mary and Florentine, Sharon (2022). "Employee Retention: 10 Strategies for Retaining Top Talent", *CIO Magazine.*

Qualtrics (2022) "What is Social Media Analytics in 2022?".

Quora (2022) "What Kinds of Colleges Does Tesla Motors Target for Internship and Job Recruiting?" Quora.

Raju, Vinothini (2021) "How Low-Code Platforms Can Help Cloud Native Developers", The New Stack.

Ranger, Steve (2022) "What is Cloud Computing? Everything You Need to Know About the Cloud Explained", ZDNet.

Ross, Sean (2022) "CapEx vs OpEx: What's the Difference?", Investopedia.

Sag, Anshel (2021) "Army Hololens 2 AR Deal", *Forbes Magazine.*

Salesforce.com (2022) "What is Digital Transformation?".

Samuels, Mark (2021) "What is Digital Transformation? Everything You Need to Know About How Technology is Reshaping Business", ZDNet.

Sant, Hitesh (2021) "10 Blockchain-as-a-Service Providers for Small to Big Businesses", Geekflare.

SAS (2022) "Digital Transformation: What It Is & Why It Matters".

Satter, Rapheal (2021) "SolarWinds Says Dealing with Hack Fallout Cost at least $18 million", Reuters.

Saviom (2021) "12 Jobs that Robots (AI) Will Replace in the Future, & 12 That Won't".

Seeking Alpha (2021) "Apple Gets Close To Their VR/AR Headset".

Sergeenkov Andrey (2019) "Artificial Intelligence is Becoming Better than Human Expertise", HackerNoon.

Shah, Samit (2021) "The Financial Impact of SolarWinds Breach", Bitsight.

SoftwareAG (2022) "What Is Process Mining?", https://www.softwareag.com/en_corporate/resources/what-is/process-mining.html.

Sozzi, Brian (2021) "McDonald's Automated Drive-Thru is Just the Latest Sign of Robots Taking Over Fast-Food", Yahoo Finance.

Swinhoe, Dan (2019) "The Biggest Data Breach Fines, Penalties and Settlements So Far", CSO Online.

Symonds, Cat (2022) "10 Types of Bias in Performance Reviews ", Factorial Blog.

Taylor, David (2022) "Data Lake vs Data Warehouse: What's the Difference?", Guru99.

Team Ecosystm (2019) "Things you need to know about Cyber Attacks, Threats & Risks", Ecosystm.

The University of Oxford (2019) "AI Technology Can Predict Heart Attacks", *Healthresearch.*

Thompson, Stuart B. and Warzel, Charlie (2021) "One Nation Tracked", *New York Times.*

TOPS Marketing (2022) "Guide to 3D Modeling", Take-Off Professionals.

Torman, Matt (2022) "Digital Transformation and the Downfall of Sears", Cleo.

Tozzi, Christopher (2021) "Top Regulatory Compliance Frameworks for 2021", Precisely.

Trend Micro (2020) "The New Norm", Trend Micro Research.

Twin, Alexandra (2022) "Core Competencies", Investopedia.

2 Steps Team (2020) "The Pervasive IT Failure Problem in the Financial Services Industry".

Valuer.ai (2022) "50 Brands that Failed to Innovate", Valuer.ai.

van Duin, Stefan and Bakhshi, Naser (2017) "Artificial Intelligence Defined", Deloitte.

Vlastelica, Ryan (2017) "Automation Could Impact 375 Million Jobs by 2030", MarketWatch.

Wealth Quint Team (2022) "15 Best Metaverse Business Ideas", Wealth Quint.

Webroot (2022) "What are Bots, Botnets and Zombies?", Webroot.

Weins, Kim (2020) "IT Spending by Industry", Flexera.

Welsh, Oli (2022) "The Metaverse, Explained", Polygon.

Wessel, David (2018) "Is Lack of Competition Strangling the U.S. Economy?", *Harvard Business Review.*

Westar (2022) "Top 10 Practical Cybersecurity Strategies for Businesses", Westar.

Whitehouse, Mark and Rojanasakul, Mira (2017) "Find Out If Your Job Will Be Automated", Bloomberg.

Wikipedia (2022) "Augmented Reality", https://en.wikipedia.org/wiki/Augmented_reality_2022.

Wikipedia (2022) "Business Model Canvas", https://en.wikipedia.org/wiki/Business_Model_Canvas.

Wikipedia (2022) "Business Processes", https://en.wikipedia.org/wiki/Business_process.

Wikipedia (2022) "Business Process Modeling", https://en.wikipedia.org/wiki/Business_process_modeling.

Wikipedia (2022) "DARPA", https://en.wikipedia.org/wiki/DARPA.

Wikipedia (2022) "Digital Transformation", https://en.wikipedia.org/wiki/Digital_transformation.

Wikipedia (2022) "Ken Olson", https://en.wikipedia.org/wiki/Ken_Olsen.

Wikipedia (2022) "Robotics", https://en.wikipedia.org/wiki/Robotics.

Wikipedia (2022) "Second Life", https://en.wikipedia.org/wiki/Second_Life.

Wikipedia (2022) "Virtual Reality", https://en.wikipedia.org/wiki/Virtual_reality.

Wilson, Sonsini, Goodrich and Rosati. (2019) "Wilson Sonsini Adds to Government Investigations Practice." Wilson Sonsini Goodrich & Rosati.

YouTube (2006) https://www.youtube.com/watch?v=YpBPavEDQCk

Zuboof, Shoshona (2019) *"The Age of Surveillance Capitalism: The Fight for a Human Future at the New Frontier of Power"*, NY: Public Affairs.

INDEX